EASTERN FRONT FROM

RED ARMY ARMOUR
IN COMBAT

EDITED AND INTRODUCED BY
BOB CARRUTHERS

Pen & Sword
MILITARY

This edition published in 2013 by
Pen & Sword Military
An imprint of
Pen & Sword Books Ltd
47 Church Street
Barnsley
South Yorkshire
S70 2AS

First published in Great Britain in 2012 in digital format by
Coda Books Ltd.

ISBN 978 1 78159 229 8

A CIP catalogue record for this book is
available from the British Library

Printed and bound by CPI Group (UK) Ltd, Croydon, CR0 4YY

Pen & Sword Books Ltd incorporates the Imprints of Pen & Sword Aviation, Pen &
Sword Family History, Pen & Sword Maritime, Pen & Sword Military, Pen &
Sword Discovery, Pen & Sword Politics, Pen & Sword Atlas, Pen & Sword
Archaeology, Wharncliffe Local History, Wharncliffe True Crime, Wharncliffe
Transport, Pen & Sword Select, Pen & Sword Military Classics, Leo Cooper, The
Praetorian Press, Claymore Press, Remember When, Seaforth Publishing and
Frontline Publishing

For a complete list of Pen & Sword titles please contact
PEN & SWORD BOOKS LIMITED
47 Church Street, Barnsley, South Yorkshire, S70 2AS, England
E-mail: enquiries@pen-and-sword.co.uk
Website: www.pen-and-sword.co.uk

CONTENTS

INTRODUCTION

This book forms part of the series entitled 'Eastern Front from Primary Sources.' The aim is to provide the reader with a varied range of materials drawn from original writings covering the strategic, operational and tactical aspects of the battles of Hitler's war in the east. The concept behind the series is to provide the well-read and knowledgeable reader with an interesting compilation of related primary sources which together build a picture of a particular aspect of the titanic struggle on the Eastern Front.

I am pleased to report that the series has been well received and it is a pleasure to be able to bring original primary sources to the attention of an interested readership. I particularly enjoy discovering new primary sources, and I am pleased to be able to present them unadorned and unvarnished to a sophisticated audience. The sources speak for themselves and the readership I strive to serve is the increasingly well informed community of reader/historians which needs no editorial lead and can draw its own conclusions. I am well aware that our community is constantly striving to discover new nuggets of information, and I trust that with this volume I have managed to stimulate fresh enthusiasm and that some of these articles will provoke readers

Left to right: A-8 (BT-7M), A-20, T-34 Model 1940, T-34 Model 1941

to research further down these lines of investigation, and perhaps cause established views to be challenged once more. I am aware at all times in compiling these materials that our relentless pursuit of more and better historical information is at the core our common passion. I trust that this selection will contribute to that search and will help all of us to better comprehend and understand the bewildering events of the last century.

The centre piece of this volume is the often overlooked US Army study 'Small Unit Actions During the German Campaign in Russia', a series of post war debriefs written for the US Army Historical department. It is highly illuminating and gives a good insight into the struggles of the Wehrmacht and its Panzers against the Soviets and their tank crews. The first year of the war saw the Russians suffering heavy losses in desperate attempts to stem the German tide which threatened to engulf them while at the same time they were trying to carry through fundamental changes in their armored tactics and equipment, but by 1943 the Germans were on the back foot against the seemingly never-ending supply of T-34 tanks and personnel.

In order to produce an interesting compilation giving a flavour of events at the tactical level I have returned once more to the US Intelligence series of pamphlets, which contain an intriguing series of contemporary articles on Russian armour and tactics. I find this series of pamphlets particularly fascinating as they are written in the present tense and, as such, provide us with a sense of what was happening at the face of battle as events unfolded.

Thank you very much for buying this volume, I hope you find something new and interesting in these pages and I sincerely hope it earns its place in your library.

Bob Carruthers
Edinburgh 2012.

SMALL UNIT ACTIONS DURING THE GERMAN CAMPAIGN IN RUSSIA: ARMOR

In 1941 the Russian armored command was in the process of reorganizing and converting to new equipment. Only selected personnel were assigned to this arm of the service, and the outdated heavy and light tanks were being replaced with medium models, primarily T34's, which mounted a 76-mm. gun and were exceptionally fast and powerful.

Before 1941 the principal function of the Russian tank unit was to support the infantry. The successes achieved by German armor during the blitzkrieg in Poland, France, and the Balkans led the Russians to a reevaluation of their doctrine affecting armor, and the Russian planners turned to the idea of using armor in a strategic role along the German lines.

During this transitional period the Russian armored command was suddenly confronted with the German invasion. The first year of the war saw the Russians suffering heavy losses in desperate attempts to stem the tide which threatened to engulf them while at the same time they were trying to carry through fundamental changes in their armored tactics and equipment.

In hastily passing from one stage to the next, Russian armored tactics and techniques developed along lines that seemed, at least to the German foe, entirely unorthodox. It was this very unorthodoxy that baffled the Germans and enabled the Russians to achieve successes, which began to sap the German strength long before Russian armor reached its full effectiveness. At the beginning of the campaign the Russians were forced to commit their armor piecemeal, usually in units no larger than a regiment. By early 1942 the independent tank brigade appeared on the field of battle, and eventually the Russians organized armored armies.

Destroyed Soviet T-34 tanks next to the Woroschilowka-Stalingrad railway, 1942.

The T34 was constantly improved during the war years, particularly with regard to its radio and sighting equipment, its armor, and, above all, its armament, which was eventually changed to an 85-mm. gun.

The technological improvements in Russian tanks were the result of many factors. The developments in German armor were without doubt known to the Russians, sometimes even in the blueprint stage. Captured German tanks became available early in the war, as did the latest United States and British thought on tank design. Of all the factors involved, it was perhaps the delivery of materiel under lend-lease agreements that had the most important impact on Russian tank construction.

The imbalance which resulted from the simultaneous effort to attain both technical perfection and tactical skill was most obvious in the conduct of battle by the small unit. In one action the Russians might demonstrate a conspicuous lack of flexibility, while in another they might prove masters in maneuvering mobile units. The records show instances where tank strength was woefully wasted, and, on the other hand, an example of how a single Russian tank tied down an entire German combat team for 48 hours.

In the actions selected for the purpose of this study there is no pattern that lends itself to generalization. If they do convey a unified impression, it is that the Russian is aware of the need for constant changes in armored tactics to keep in step with technological improvements, and that he is extremely flexible in the application of these tactics. He is a master of camouflage. He will dig in his tank as readily as he digs in an antitank gun, and will usually succeed in removing it after it has been bypassed. He seeks ever to preserve mobility. He will hit and run; he will hit and stay; he will use his tanks as decoys, for traps, in ambush. He will always do the unexpected. The Russian tanker, who knew his native soil better than he knew his field manuals, eventually drove the German invaders all the way back to Berlin.

The following small unit actions show clearly the way in which the Russians overcame their early mistakes and developed an effective fighting force. In these examples of armored combat, descriptive details are fewer than in infantry engagements at a similar level. This comparative lack of detailed information reflects the very nature of tank warfare, which takes place at a rapid pace and therefore offers fewer clues to permit a reconstruction of events. The absence of details, however, in no way diminishes the intrinsic value of the material presented.

THE ARMORED ROADBLOCK
(JUNE 1941)

When Germany launched her attack against Russia on the morning of 22 June 1941, Army Group North jumped off from positions along the border separating East Prussia from Lithuania. On D plus 1 the 6th Panzer Division, which was part of Army Group North, was ordered to occupy the Lithuanian town of Rossienie and thence to seize the two vehicular bridges across the Dubysa River north-east of the town (map below). After Rossienie was taken the division was split into Combat Teams R and S, which were to establish two bridgeheads, Combat Team R being assigned the bridge nearest Lydavenai, a

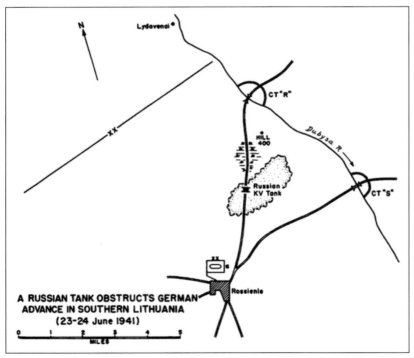

A Russian tank obstructs German advance in southern Lithuania
(23-24 June 1941)

village situated almost due north of Rossienie. By early afternoon both columns had crossed the river and contact was established between the two bridgeheads.

Mopping-up operations around its bridgehead netted Combat Team R a number of prisoners, about 20 of whom, including a first lieutenant, were loaded onto a truck for evacuation to Rossienie. One German sergeant was placed in charge of the group.

About half-way to Rossienie the truck driver suddenly noticed a Russian tank astride the road. As the truck slowed to a halt, the prisoners pounced upon the driver and the sergeant, and the Russian lieutenant lunged for the sergeant's machine pistol. In the struggle that ensued, the powerful German sergeant freed his right arm and struck the lieutenant such a hard blow that he and several other Russians were knocked down by the impact. Before the prisoners could close in again, the sergeant freed his other arm and fired the machine pistol into the midst of the group. The effect of the fire was devastating. Only the lieutenant and a few others escaped; the rest were killed.

The sergeant and the driver returned to the bridgehead with the empty truck and informed their commanding officer that the only supply route to the bridgehead was blocked by a heavy tank of the KV type. The Russian tank crew had meanwhile severed telephone communication between the bridgehead and the division command post.

The Russian plan was not clear. In estimating the situation, the bridgehead commander felt that because of the encounter with the tank an attack against the rear of the bridgehead was to be expected; accordingly, he organized his force immediately for all-around defense. An antitank battery was moved to high ground near the command post, one of the howitzer batteries reversed its field of fire so as to face southwestward, and the engineer company prepared to mine the road and the area in front of the defense position. The tank battalion, which was deployed in a forest southeast of the bridgehead, prepared for a counterattack.

During the rest of the day the tank did not move. The next morning, 24 June, the division tried to send 12 supply trucks from Rossienie to the bridgehead. All 12 were destroyed by the Russian tank. A German reconnaissance patrol sent out around noon could find no evidence that a general Russian attack was impending.

The Germans could not evacuate their wounded from the bridgehead. Every attempt to bypass the tank failed because any vehicle that drove off the road got stuck in the mud and fell prey to Russians hiding in the surrounding forest.

On the same day, an antitank battery with 50-mm. guns was ordered to work its way forward and destroy the tank. The battery confidently accepted this mission. As the first guns approached to within 1,000 yards of the KV, it remained in place, apparently unaware of the German movement. Within the next 30 minutes the entire battery, well camouflaged, had worked its way to within firing range.

Still the tank did not move. It was such a perfect target that the battery commander felt that it must have been damaged and abandoned, but he nevertheless decided to fire. The first round, from about 600 yards, was a direct hit. A second and a third round followed. The troops assembled on the hill near the combat team's command post cheered like spectators at a shooting match. Still the tank did not move.

By the time that the eighth hit was scored, the Russian tank crew had discovered the position of the firing battery. Taking careful aim, they silenced the entire battery with a few 76-mm. shells, which destroyed two guns and damaged the others. Having suffered heavy casualties, the gun crews were withdrawn to avoid further losses. Not until after dark could the damaged guns be recovered.

Since the 50-mm. antitank guns had failed to pierce the 3-

German 50-mm. antitank gun in position.

inch armor, it was decided that only the 88-mm. flak gun with its armor-piercing shells would be effective. That same afternoon an 88-mm. flak gun was pulled out of its position near Rossienie and cautiously moved up in the direction of the tank, which was then facing the bridgehead. Well camouflaged with branches and concealed by the burned-out German trucks lining the road, the gun safely reached the edge of the forest and stopped 900 yards from the tank.

Just as the German crew was maneuvering the gun into position, the tank swung its turret and fired, blasting the flak gun into a ditch. Every round scored a direct hit, and the gun crew suffered heavy casualties. Machinegun fire from the tank made it impossible to retrieve the gun or the bodies of the German dead. The Russians had allowed the gun to approach undisturbed, knowing that it was no threat while in motion and that the nearer it came the more certain was its destruction.

Meanwhile, the bridgehead's supplies were running so low that the troops had to eat their canned emergency rations. A staff meeting was therefore called to discuss further ways and means of dealing with the tank. It was decided that an engineer detachment should attempt to blow it up in a night operation.

When the engineer company commander asked for 12 volunteers, the men were so anxious to succeed where others had failed that the entire company of 120 volunteered. He ordered the company to count off and chose every tenth man. The detachment was told about its mission, given detailed instructions, and issued explosives and other essential equipment.

Under cover of darkness the detachment moved out, led by the company commander. The route followed was a little-used sandy path which led past Hill 400 and into the woods that surrounded the location of the tank. As the engineers approached the tank, they could distinguish its contours in the pale starlight. After removing their boots, they crawled to the edge of the road to observe the tank more closely and to decide how to approach their task.

Suddenly there was a noise from the opposite side of the road, and the movement of several dark figures could be discerned. The Germans thought that the tank crew had dismounted. A moment later, however, the sound of tapping against the side of the tank was heard and the turret was slowly raised. The figures handed something to the tank crew, and the sound of clinking dishes could be heard. The Germans concluded that these were partisans bringing food to the tank crew. The temptation to overpower them was great, and ,it probably would have been a simple matter. Such an action, however, would have alerted the tank crew and perhaps have wrecked the entire scheme. After about an hour the partisans withdrew, and the tank turret was closed.

It was about 0100 before the engineers could finally get to work. They attached one explosive charge to the track and the side of the tank and withdrew after lighting the fuse. A violent explosion ripped the air. The last echoes of the roar had hardly faded away when the tank's machineguns began to sweep the area with fire. The tank did not move. Its tracks appeared to be damaged, but no close examination could be made in the face of the intense machinegun fire. Doubtful of success, the engineer detachment returned to the bridgehead and made its report. One of the twelve men was listed as missing.

Shortly before daylight a second explosion was heard from the vicinity of the tank, again followed by the sound of machinegun fire; then, after some time had passed, silence reigned once more.

Later that same morning, as the personnel around the command post of Combat Team R were resuming their normal duties, they noticed a barefoot soldier with a pair of boots under his arm crossing the bivouac area. When the commanding officer halted the lone wanderer, all eyes turned to watch. The colonel was heard asking the soldier for an explanation of his unmilitary appearance. Soon the sound of their voices became inaudible as the two principals in this little drama engaged in earnest conversation.

As they talked, the colonel's face brightened, and after a few minutes he offered the soldier a cigarette, which the latter accepted, visibly embarrasssed. Finally, the colonel patted the soldier on the back, shook his hand, and the two parted, the soldier still carrying his boots. The curiosity of the onlookers was not satisfied until the order of the day was published, together with the following extract from the barefoot soldier's report:

I was detailed as an observer for the detachment that was sent to blow up the Russian tank. After all preparations had been made, the company commander and I attached a charge of about double the normal size to the tank track, and I returned to the ditch which was my observation post. The ditch was deep enough to offer protection against splinters, and I waited there to observe the effect of the explosion. The tank, however, covered the area with sporadic machinegun fire following the explosion. After about an hour, when everything had quieted down, I crept to the tank and examined the place where I had attached the charge. Hardly half of the track was destroyed, and I could find no other damage to the tank. I returned to the assembly point only to find that the detachment had departed. While looking for

Russian KV tank demolished by the Germans, July 1941

my boots I found that another demolition charge had been left behind. I took it, returned to the tank, climbed onto it, and fastened the charge to the gun barrel in the hope of destroying at least that part of the tank, the charge not being large enough to do any greater damage. I crept under the tank and detonated the charge. The tank immediately covered the edge of the forest with machinegun fire which did not cease until dawn, when I was finally able to crawl out from under the tank. When I inspected the effect of the demolition, I saw, to my regret, that the charge I had used was too weak. The gun was only slightly damaged. Upon returning to the assembly point, I found a pair of boots, which I tried to put on, but they were too small. Someone had apparently taken my boots by mistake. That is why I returned barefoot and late to my company.

Here was the explanation of the missing man, the morning explosion, and the second burst of machinegun fire.

Three German attempts had failed. The tank still blocked the road and could fire at will. Plan 4, calling for an attack on the tank by dive bombers, had to be canceled when it was learned that no such aircraft could be made available. Whether the dive bombers could have succeeded in scoring a direct hit on the tank is questionable, but it is certain that anything short of that would not have eliminated it.

Plan 5 involved a calculated risk and called for deceiving the tank crew. It was hoped that in this way German losses would be kept to a minimum. A feint frontal attack was to be executed by a tank formation approaching from various points in the forest east of the road while another 88-mm. gun was to be brought up from Rossienie to destroy the tank. The terrain was quite suitable for this operation; the forest was lightly wooded and presented no obstacle to tank maneuver.

The German armor deployed and attacked the Russian tank from three sides. The Russian crew, clearly excited, swung the gun turret around and around in an effort to hit the German tanks which kept up a continuous fire from the woods.

Meanwhile, the 88-mm. gun took up a position to the rear of the tank. The very first round was a direct hit and, as the crew tried to turn the gun to the rear, a second and a third shell struck home. Mortally wounded, the tank remained motionless, but did not burn. Four more 88-mm. armor-piercing shells hit their mark. Then, following the last hit, the tank gun rose straight up as if, even now, to defy its attackers.

The Germans closest to the tank dismounted and moved in on their victim. To their great surprise they found that but two of the 88-mm. shells had pierced the tank armor, the five others having made only deep dents. Eight blue marks, made by direct hits of the 50-mm. antitank guns, were found. The results of the engineer attack had amounted to only a damaged track and a slight dent in the gun barrel. No trace of the fire from the German tanks could be found.

Driven by curiosity, the Germans climbed onto the tank and tried to open the turret, but to no avail. Suddenly, the gun barrel started to move again and most of the Germans scattered. Quickly, two engineers dropped hand grenades through the hole made by the hit on the lower part of the turret. A dull explosion followed, and the turret cover blew off. Inside were the mutilated bodies of the crew. The Germans had come off poorly in their first encounter with a KV at this point of the front, one single tank having succeeded in blocking the supply route of a strong German force for 48 hours.

GERMAN ARMORED ENGINEERS CAPTURE TWO BRIDGES (JUNE 1941)

While elements of the 6th Panzer Division were thus momentarily delayed, the 8th Panzer Division, which was also part of Army Group North, spearheaded the German attack farther south, taking the Russians completely by surprise. The 8th Panzer Division sped northeastward in the face of sporadic and constantly diminishing enemy resistance, leaving Russian units at its flanks and rear to be mopped up later by the German infantry. On the evening of 24 June the division reached Smelyney a village on the Lithuanian-Latvian border, 12 miles southwest of Dvinsk. It had advanced over an excellent highway through open and gently rolling terrain.

Late on 24 June the division commander made an estimate of this situation. The division's immediate objective was the city of Dvinsk, situated on the north bank of the Dvina (map overleaf). However, in order to capture the city the division first had to seize the 2 bridges spanning the river, which was approximately 250 yards wide in this area. While the highway bridge was needed for the division's advance, the other, a railroad bridge situated about a mile downstream, was to be used as an alternate should the Russians succeed in demolishing the highway bridge. German air reconnaissance had indicated that the Russians intended to defend Dvinsk and that the two bridges across the Dvina had been prepared for demolition. The destruction of these bridges, however, would delay the division's advance and thus upset the Army Group's timetable. Consequently, the two bridges had to be seized in a surprise raid before the Russians could destroy them. The division commander decided to act without delay and ordered the

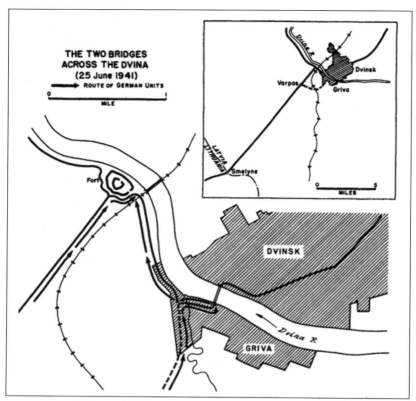

The two bridges across the Dvina (25 June 1941)

commander of the division's advance guard and Lieutenant Schneider, CO of Company Cy 59th Armored Engineer Battalion, to report to his CP immediately. After the two officers arrived there, he briefly outlined the general situation and then issued the following verbal orders:

One platoon of Company C, divided into four assault detachments, will launch a surprise attack against the two bridges at Dvinsk. The detachments will jump off at 0130 on 25 June and head for the bridges in the four Russian trucks that the division captured earlier today. The Russians must be led to believe that the trucks are friendly, so that the assault detachments can get within striking distance of the bridges without being challenged.

Once the detachments have reached the bridges, they

20

will immediately cut all cables leading to the bridges from both banks to prevent the enemy from setting off the demolition charges electrically, cut all detonating cords leading to the charges, and defend the bridges against Russian counterattacks.

The main body of Company C will also jump off at 0130, but will proceed somewhat more slowly so as to arrive at the bridges about 15 minutes after the assault detachments, which it will relieve. Company C will be followed by the division's advance guard, which will arrive at the highway bridge at 0305. Since the highway bridge should be firmly in German hands by this time, the advance guard, consisting of one armored infantry battalion and one tank battalion, will cross over into Dvinsk and spearhead the division's northeastward advance.

Gentlemen, I have confidence in your ability to execute this difficult mission successfully and wish you luck. If there are no questions, that is all.

Preparations for the impending mission were quickly made. Schneider organized the 4th Platoon of his company into four assault detachments, each consisting of 10 men equipped with machineguns, submachine guns, hand grenades, and wire cutters.

The main body of Company C was to march in the following order:

1st and 2d Platoons, each equipped with five special engineer tanks. These vehicles were Mark II tanks, each armed with a 20-mm gun and a machinegun. At the back of each tank a special boom had been mounted for the purpose of depositing demolition charges and removing obstacles.

The seven half-tracks of the 4th Platoon, equipped with frame-type rocket projectors, were to follow the first two platoons. On the march the half-tracks were to be occupied only by the drivers, since the other men of the 4th Platoon were to form the assault detachments.

The 5th Platoon, composed of combat engineers equipped with demolition charges, was to follow in trucks.

Company C's 3d Platoon was engaged in bridge construction elsewhere and was not available for the operation.

Company C moved out of its bivouac near Smelyne at 0130. With their headlights on, the trucks carrying the assault detachments sped northeastward at 40 m. p. h. over the hard-surfaced road in the direction of Dvinsk. The company's tanks and half-tracks followed the trucks at a lower rate of speed. Initially, everything proceeded according to plan. The assault detachments did not encounter any Russians and continued toward the bridges at unabated speed.

At Varpas, 2 miles from the river, the first three trucks turned east and continued toward the highway bridge, while the fourth truck headed straight for the railroad bridge. The detachments passed several Russian infantrymen, but the latter apparently assumed that the trucks were friendly and did not challenge them.

a. The Struggle for the Highway Bridge.

After turning east at Varpas, the three trucks continued on at full speed, reaching Griva on the south bank of the Dvina at 0215. The southwestern outskirts of Griva were occupied by a Russian rear guard of about 50 men, who let the trucks pass through. Only a short distance separated the assault detachments from the bridge, and the men became tense. At the approach to the bridge Russian sentries blocked the road and challenged the first truck, which then slowed down. It seemed to the detachment commander that his luck had finally run out. Since deception was no longer possible, only quick action could save the day. The driver of the first truck pulled up close to the Russian sentries as if to stop. Then, at the last moment, he stepped on the gas, and the truck lurched forward with a roar and headed across the bridge, followed by a second truck. A few of the Russians standing in the path of the trucks managed to jump out of the

Tests of the first T-34 on the Karelian isthmus. 1940

way. Others, less fortunate, were run over. Those that were able to do so, leaped to the aid of their injured comrades. In the confusion, little attention was paid to the third truck, which had halted at the approach to the bridge. At a given signal, its occupants suddenly jumped the dazed Russians with knives and bayonets, killing them all. Four of the men then rushed to the bridge and cut all the wires they could locate. The first truck meanwhile succeeded in crossing the bridge without being attacked; the second, however, which had stopped briefly at the middle of the bridge to drop off a wire-cutting detail, received small-arms fire from the north bank and quickly moved on to the far end of the bridge where it joined the first. The wire-cutting detail had barely completed its work when enemy machineguns and antitank guns on the north bank of the Dvina opened fire, pinning the men down. The two detachments at the north end of the bridge also drew fire and suffered their first casualties. At 0230 the Russians launched a strong counterattack in an attempt to drive the two detachments from the north end of the bridge. In the ensuing close combat both sides suffered heavy losses. Ten minutes after the trucks had first rolled onto the bridge the Russian rear guard arrived from Griva and attacked the detachment at the south end. However, despite their numerical superiority, the Russians were unable to dislodge the three assault detachments from the bridge, although they did prevent the German engineers from conducting a systematic search for the demolition charges. Even though the Germans had cut all cables on the bridge, making it impossible for the Russians to set off the charges electrically, there was still the danger that they would set them off by means of detonating cords if they succeeded in getting onto the bridge.

At 0240, just as the assault detachments began to run short of ammunition and hand grenades, they were relieved by the main body of the company. During the 20 minutes of fighting the three assault detachments, which altogether numbered 30 men at the outset, had suffered heavy casualties. One officer, one NCO, and three privates were killed, and four men were wounded.

With the arrival of the main body of the company, tanks of the 1st and 2d Platoons went into position on the south bank and began to fire at Russian troops in Dvinsk. Ten minutes later the halftracks of the 4th Platoon joined the special engineer tanks and fired rockets into Dvinsk. Large fires soon broke out in the city.

After a brief struggle the remnants of the Russian rear guard on the south bank surrendered. A strong Russian force, which had assembled north of the bridge for a counterattack, was caught in the German barrage and dispersed before the attack could get under way.

By 0255, when the division's advance guard arrived, Company C had accomplished its mission of seizing the highway bridge intact. At 0305 the division's advance guard began to cross the bridge and push on into Dvinsk against fierce Russian resistance.

There remained only one more task to be carried out by Company C: the removal of the demolition charges on the bridge. A hasty check indicated that the Russians had prepared each of the three spans for demolition. However, the check did not reveal any charges at the piers.

While a detail was preparing to remove the charges, one of the men suddenly noticed a puff of smoke nearby and discovered that a Russian had crawled onto the bridge, apparently unnoticed, and had lighted a detonating cord. Jumping forward, the engineer wrenched the cord from the charge only 10 seconds before the explosion would have taken place. At almost the same time a similar incident occurred near the north end of the bridge. Here the detonation was also prevented just in time.

With the company's mission at the highway bridge accomplished, Lieutenant Schneider was able to turn his attention to the railroad bridge, where the noise of battle was audible, indicating that the 4th Assault Detachment had run into trouble. Schneider dispatched Company C's 2d and 5th Platoons to that bridge by way of the road which ran parallel to the river.

b. The Struggle for the Railroad Bridge.

When the first three assault detachments, en route to the highway bridge, turned east at Varpas shortly after 0200, the other truck continued north on the main highway, which led directly to the railroad bridge. Several hundred yards short of the bridge, at the intersection with the road that parallels the river, there was an old fort whose outer wall the truck had to pass. As the vehicle turned right onto the river road it received small-arms fire from the fort. In a matter of seconds the truck caught fire and was hastily abandoned. The detachment then attempted to fight its way toward the bridge on foot, a distance of some 500 yards. However, the men were soon pinned down by the Russian fire, despite which they slowly and laboriously crawled toward the bridge. Just as the detachment had inched close enough to rush the bridge, there was a terrific explosion. Apparently aware of German intentions, the Russians had detonated charges attached to the steel piers. As the smoke cleared, it became evident that the demolition had not been very effective. The bridge was still intact. The wood planking and the rail ties had, however, caught fire, and there was danger that the fire might set off additional charges, which would normally be placed beneath certain girders of the truss sections. Quick action on the part of the assault detachment was therefore necessary if the fire was to be extinguished and the bridge saved.

At 0330 the 2d and 5th Platoons of Company C arrived at the east entrance to the fort, which was blocked by a heavy steel gate. Since the fire at the railroad bridge was still unchecked and fire-fighting equipment could not be brought up as long as the Russians kept the bridge under fire, the two platoons were ordered to take the fort by direct assault.

The men of the 5th Platoon, who had dismounted and tried to place a demolition charge next to the gate, drew heavy Russian small arms fire. An estimate of the situation indicated that it would be inadvisable to approach the gate without the protection of armor. Accordingly, one of the 2d Platoon's special engineer tanks was ordered to back up to the gate and lower a 110-pound HE charge from its boom. As soon as the charge had been deposited and the tank had moved to a safe distance, the charge was set off. The terrific explosion destroyed the gate and stunned the Russians in the immediate vicinity. However, as the German tanks advanced through the breach, they again drew fire. Their progress was further impeded by a second wall, whose gate, also of steel, was on the side facing the river. Again a special engineer tank had to be brought up with a 110-pound HE charge, which was set off with the same results as the first. At this point a few Russians surrendered. The remainder of the garrison, about 20 in number, continued to resist from the CP, which was located in a structure at the very center of the fort. While the Russians in the fort were trying desperately to repulse the German attack, Company C's fire-fighting equipment proceeded to the railroad bridge and quickly extinguished the blaze. Using shaped charges and hand grenades the 5th Platoon finally succeeded in driving the Russians from their last foothold within the fort. At 0400 the fight for the fort came to an end. Of the company of Russians that had held the fort, 70 had been killed or wounded and 30 taken prisoner.

The entire action had been carried out with great speed, only half an hour having elapsed between the initial assault on the fort and its capture. When interrogated, Russians captured at the fort stated that they had been ordered to hold out as long as possible, even if the bridge were demolished. They were to keep the Germans from moving up bridge equipment over the highway and to delay the German advance as long as possible.

With both bridges firmly in German hands, Company C's mission was accomplished. In the fierce fighting which continued until evening the 8th Panzer Division captured Dvinsk and continued its northeastward advance toward Leningrad.

The preceding example illustrates to what extent the commitment of armor in situations where speed is imperative can result in major successes. The seizure of the two bridges at Dvinsk was possible mainly because the four captured Russian trucks were sent ahead of the main body of Company C, thus taking the Russians by surprise and preventing them from demolishing the bridges before the Germans could reach them.

The selection of Company C for this mission was justified because its special engineer tanks and half-tracks had sufficient fire power to pin the Russians down north of the highway bridge and pave the way for the division's advance into Dvinsk. During the fighting for the fort, the special engineer tanks once more proved invaluable in destroying the two gates. Only armor could get close enough to the gates to place the demolition charges in the face of the heavy Russian small-arms fire.

RUSSIAN TANK TRAP
(JULY 1941)

By the beginning of July 1941 the 3d Panzer Division, which was part of Army Group Center, had reached the Dnepr River north of Zhlobin and was preparing to attack across the river. On 6 July the division's tank regiment, then in reserve, was ordered to relieve an infantry division which had encountered strong Russian resistance while attacking Zhlobin from the southwest. The infantry attack had bogged down about 2 1/2 miles southwest of the town (map below).

The terrain around Zhlobin was gently rolling grassland alternating with swampy ground. The weather was warm and sunny.

The tank regiment commander decided to employ 2 battalions, each with about 40 tanks. According to his plan the

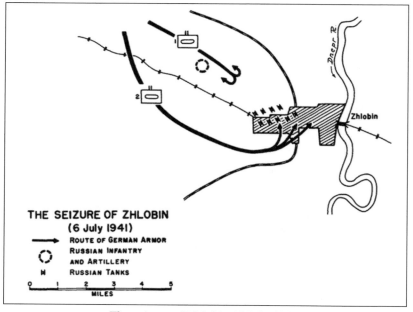

The seizure of Zhlobin (6 July 1941)

28

1st Battalion was to advance straight toward Zhlobin. The 2d Battalion was to follow the 1st up to a point approximately 1 mile from the Russian MLR northwest of Zhlobin, turn southward, cross the railroad tracks, and drive southeastward to smash the Russian forces which—so he presumed—were holding positions immediately south of the town. This two-pronged thrust would put him in possession of Zhlobin and simultaneously relieve the German infantry.

The march column advanced according to plan. About 2 1/2 miles northwest of Zhlobin the 1st Battalion penetrated the Russian MLR against weak resistance, overran some Russian infantry elements, and then bypassed an artillery battery. Suddenly, when the lead tanks were only a mile from the outskirts of the town, they received devastating fire from Russian tanks which had been cleverly concealed among houses, farmyards, and barns at the edge of the town. The Russian tanks, lying in ambush, had held their fire until the last moment. When the 1st Battalion tanks veered to escape the onslaught, they received point-blank fire from the artillery battery they had bypassed. The Russian artillerymen had turned their pieces on the German battalion. In all the Germans lost 22 tanks as a result of this ambush.

The 2d Battalion had meanwhile received desperate calls for assistance over the radio, but could not come to the rescue because the high railroad embankment obstructed its path. The battalion commander therefore decided to bring relief by a direct thrust on Zhlobin. Upon finding the Russian left flank open, the battalion entered the town from the south and destroyed 25 of the 30 Russian tanks without suffering any losses. The Russians had not expected a thrust from this direction and had devoted all their attention to fighting the 1st Battalion.

The failure of the 1st Battalion's frontal attack must be ascribed to its laxity in reconnaissance before attempting to relieve the infantry division. Moreover, tanks on an independent mission should be accompanied by armored infantry. In this instance armored infantry might have been able to capture the Russian artillery battery.

Had the 2d Battalion followed the 1st, the artillery battery could have been neutralized and immediate assistance given to the 1st Battalion. In obscure situations it is better to advance in depth in order to meet possible surprise with unfettered forces than to advance on a relatively wide front where contact may be lost and separate elements of one's forces may be pinned down. In the ambush of the 1st Battalion the discipline of the Russians, combined with their characteristic craftiness, more than compensated for their inferiority in training and equipment. An ambush is indeed an economical operation against a careless foe.

GERMAN ARMORED ENGINEERS ON THE ROAD TO LENINGRAD (AUGUST 1941)

During the last days of August 1941 Army Group North forces drove toward Leningrad from Kingisepp and from Luga. In an effort to keep open the route of withdrawal of their forces that had been defeated at Luga, the Russians put up strong resistance to the German armor thrusting eastward from Kingisepp. Continuing their relentless drive, the German panzer divisions broke through the Russian front southwest of Leningrad at several points. By that time the Russian top-level command seemed to have lost overall control of the forces employed in the vicinity of Leningrad, but individual units—probably driven by their commissars—continued to fight stubbornly.

On 28 August the 8th Panzer Division, which was assembled approximately 30 miles southeast of Kingisepp, received orders to spearhead the thrust from the southwest on the following day. By advancing via Moloskovitsy and Volosovo the division was to reach the Luga-Leningrad highway at a point south of Gatchina (map overleaf). Upon arriving at the highway the division was to turn southeastward and thus, by attacking the withdrawing Russian forces from the rear, facilitate the advance of those German infantry divisions that were fighting their way northward. Meanwhile, other German armored forces were to capture Gatchina and various objectives farther to the north on the road to Leningrad.

The terrain through which the German armor was to advance was swampy forest land. A few minor elevations afforded a good view of the surrounding countryside. At this time of the summer all highways and roads, with the exception of those leading through extremely swampy terrain, were passable for vehicular

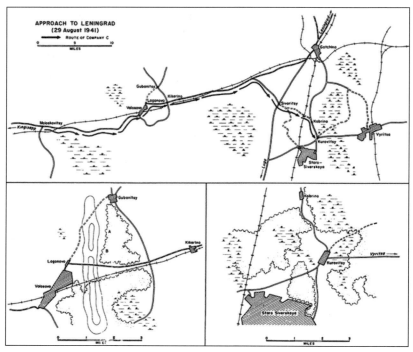

Approach to Leningrad (29 August 1941)

traffic. The sun rose at 0300.

The 8th Panzer Division moved out at 0400 on 29 August and entered Moloskovitsy during the early morning hours. Weak Russian forces entrenched at the railroad station were quickly dispersed, and the advance guard continued its march toward Volosovo. Isolated nests of resistance failed to delay the Germans.

Company C of the 59th Armored Engineer Battalion, marching at the head of the first divisional column, arrived in Volosovo at 1230 and halted for a short break. A liaison officer and motorcycle messengers maintained contact with the advance guard which, according to the latest report, had reached Kikerino at 1215.

At 1235 Lieutenant Schneider, the commander of Company C, heard machinegun and antitank gun fire from the northeast. Just as he was stepping into his vehicle with the intention of investigating the situation, a supply truck of the advance guard drove up and stopped. The driver reported that his truck column had been ambushed about 1 1/2 miles east of Volosovo. While the other truck drivers had tried to escape by accelerating their vehicles, he had turned around and headed back to notify the march column commander.

On the basis of this information Schneider ordered the 1st and 2d (Tank) Platoons to move to the road fork at Lagonovo and the 4th Platoon, consisting of rocket projectors mounted on half-tracks, to a point immediately south of that road fork. The 5th Platoon, composed of combat engineers, was to take up positions on the northeast outskirts of Volosovo. Schneider got into his vehicle and drove off in the direction of Kikerino. About 1 mile east of the Lagonovo road fork he stopped at the top of a low ridge from which he was able to observe approximately 300 Russian riflemen emerging from the west side of the woods south of Gubanitsy at a point about half a mile north of the highway (Point B). They were heading for the ridge just a few hundred yards west of the woods. Schneider also noticed that one Russian machinegun and one antitank gun were emplaced at the southwest edge of the forest. He felt certain that these must have been the weapons that had ambushed the truck column. Two burning trucks lay in the ditch along the highway about 500 yards east of his observation point. Small arms ammunition was exploding in one of the trucks.

Schneider arrived at the conclusion that the Russians were attempting to cut off the advance guard and recapture Volosovo. Quick action seemed imperative if the Russians were to be prevented from delaying the division's advance toward the Luga-Leningrad highway.

Upon his return to the Lagonovo road fork at 1305 Schneider met the march column commander who approved his plan to eliminate the Russian threat. Schneider thereupon called his platoon leaders and issued the following verbal orders:

1. Company C will immediately attack the Russian companies

approaching the ridge, disperse them, and prevent any additional Russian forces from emerging from the forest.

2. The 1st Tank Platoon will deploy immediately along the Lagonovo-Gubanitsy road midway between the two villages, lay down a smoke screen when the rocket projectors fire their salvo, and drive to Point A, which is shown on your map, at the forest's edge. The platoon will protect its own left flank.

3. The 2d Tank Platoon will assemble east of the road fork and jump off simultaneously with the 1st, directing its thrust toward point B.

4. The 4th Platoon will take up positions outside of Lagonovo and fire a salvo of 24 rockets at the two aforementioned points. It will then close up to the 2d Platoon and annihilate the Russian forces caught between the ridge and the edge of the forest. The 1st Squad of the 4th Platoon will remain in its firing position as company reserve.

5. The 5th Platoon will proceed along the highway, detruck at a point about 1,000 yards east of the road fork, occupy that stretch of the road which crosses the ridge, and form the right wing of the attack force. This platoon will also clear the southwest edge of the forest and secure the portion of the highway that borders on the forest.

6. I shall be with the 4th Platoon.

At 1330 the four platoons were assembling for the attack and Schneider was driving toward Gubanitsy. On his way he saw the first Russians coming down the west side of the ridge. They advanced in extended formation with scouts moving about 20 yards ahead of the main body. He also observed some Russians pulling antitank guns from the forest toward the ridge. Two more Russian infantry companies were just emerging from the woods at Points A and B. This second wave followed in the steps of the first.

Five minutes later the 4th Platoon fired its salvo of rockets, which landed in the center of the deploying second wave. The smoke screen laid down by the two tank platoons hid the advancing vehicles from view of the Russians who began to fire from the ridge. The tanks retaliated and the fire fight grew more intense as Company C's counterattack gained momentum.

When the smoke began to lift several minutes later, Schneider saw that the tanks had reached the crest of the ridge and that their fire was pinning down the Russian infantry, whose ranks were beginning to break. In a vain attempt to escape annihilation, individual riflemen bunched together, but were mowed down by machine-gun fire from the tanks. The Russian antitank guns stood in the middle of the field, abandoned by their crews. Isolated nests of resistance continued to fire, but their small arms were ineffective against the German tanks, which drove straight toward their designated objectives. The 5th Platoon mopped up behind the tanks, rounding up the prisoners. Remnants of the second wave that had escaped the rocket salvo tried to make their way to the woods.

By 1400 the four platoons had accomplished their missions, and the fighting was all but over when the 1st Platoon's left flank suddenly came under heavy weapons fire from the north. The platoon leader radioed that enemy infantry was attacking in company strength. Schneider immediately committed the reserve squad of the 4th Platoon plus one tank of the headquarters section and ordered that 12 rockets be fired at the Russian attack force. By 1420 the flank attack had been beaten off, and 10 minutes later Schneider informed the march column that traffic on the highway to Kikerino could be resumed. The entire operation had taken less than 2 hours. The Russian forces in the forest had suffered such heavy losses that no further attacks on German march columns were expected at that point.

In its further advance toward the Luga-Leningrad highway the 8th Panzer Division encountered little resistance. On the other hand, the German infantry divisions moving north from Luga made little progress. They were opposed by Russian forces that had not disintegrated and were therefore able to offer sustained resistance. On the evening of the same day the Luga-Leningrad highway was cut when leading elements of the 8th Panzer Division reached Sivoritsy, a village situated about 10 miles south of Gatchina.

Plans for the following day called for the division to split into two task forces. One column was to advance southward along the highway toward Luga, while the other was to drive southeastward toward Staro-Siverskaya. During the night of 29-30 August Schneider and his men were to drive via Kobrino to Kurovitsy and occupy the latter. The division commander considered Kurovitsy an important junction through which the Russians might channel reinforcements or withdraw their troops toward Vyritsa. In any event, possession of the town was important for the successful accomplishment of the division's mission to assist the advance of the infantry divisions.

With the 1st and 5th Platoons in the lead, the company drove through Kobrino without stopping and reached Kurovitsy at 2145. Here it again made contact with Russian troops when its lead tanks suddenly observed 10 trucks loaded with Russian infantry just about to pull out in the direction of Vyritsa. The German tanks immediately opened fire, but one truck escaped in the direction of Vyritsa and two more along the road leading to Staro-Siverskaya. The remaining trucks were immobilized, but most of their occupants escaped into the night, which was so dark that the Germans refrained from pursuit.

Schneider decided to organize the defense of Kurovitsy for the remainder of the night. At the southern outskirts the 1st Platoon and one squad from the 5th were to mine and block the two roads to Staro-Siverskaya. The 2d Platoon less one tank was to obstruct the road to Vyritsa at the eastern outskirts. Another squad of the 5th Platoon was to take up positions at the forest's edge about a mile down the same road and mine the roadbed at that point. The 5th Platoon, less the two above-mentioned squads, was to move to the forest's edge northeast of the village and establish an outpost line. The remaining combat forces were to form the company's reserves and assemble in the northern and northwestern parts of the village. The service vehicles had stayed behind in Kobrino. Schneider felt that these measures would provide adequate security against a sudden attack which, despite the prevailing quiet, was expected at any time.

At 0015 the 2d Platoon reported hearing the noise of tracked vehicles approaching from the direction of Vyritsa. Forty-five minutes later a Russian truck proceeding north from Staro-Siverskaya hit a mine. One wounded Russian officer was captured and two men were killed; the rest escaped.

At 0230 the 2d Platoon sent another message indicating that the noise of tracked vehicles could be heard, this time nearer than before. Shortly thereafter the noise stopped and quiet reigned until 0400, when the 2d Platoon reported that its platoon leader had just been shot from ambush. Half an hour later the 1st Platoon sent a message stating that five trucks were approaching from Staro-Siverskaya and soon afterward Schneider, at his CP just northwest of the village, heard the noice of fighting, which seemed to be coming from the southern outskirts. He soon found out that the trucks had been immobilized after hitting the German mines. While German machineguns fired at them from pointblank range, about thirty Russians had jumped off the trucks and sought cover on both sides of the road. Two of the German tanks finally dispersed them, and the few Russians who managed to escape withdrew to the nearby woods.

A few minutes later isolated small-arms fire coming from within the village could be heard. A messenger arrived on foot at Schneider's CP to report that he had been attacked two blocks down the main street and forced to abandon his damaged motorcycle. The noise of battle gradually came closer, when the 2d Platoon radioed that it was receiving fire from houses on the eastern outskirts. Schneider realized that immediate counter-measures had to be taken and ordered the 5th Platoon to assemble all of its squads on the northern outskirts and to comb out the village from north to south.

At 0510 the 5th Platoon, supported by two tanks, began to advance southward astride the main street. Bitter house-to-house fighting developed. The approaching Germans were met by sniper fire from houses, hedges, and hay stacks. The armored engineers used concentrated charges, hand grenades, and machinegun and tank-gun fire to clear one house after another. Some of the Russian soldiers feigned death only to resume fighting as soon as the Germans had passed.

The struggle within Kurovitsy reached its climax at 0520. Twenty minutes later the eastern section had been combed out and 10 prisoners were brought in. To clean out the western part, however, Schneider had to employ all his reserves. Each hay and straw stack had to be sprayed with bullets. Every Russian had to be ferreted out if he was not to resume the fight by sniping at the Germans. Those Russians who surrendered did so only because there was no other way out. By 0600 Russian resistance within Kurovitsy had collapsed.

Even though the town was now firmly in German hands, Schneider felt that further attacks from the direction of Staro-Siverskaya were possible and he therefore strengthened the 1st Platoon. At 0750, while Schneider was inspecting the defenses at the southern outskirts, the 2d Platoon reported the noise of tanks approaching from Vyritsa. Shortly thereafter the first shells landed in the center of Kurovitsy. Just as Schneider was about to leave for the new danger area on the eastern outskirts, Russian infantry, emerging in company strength from the woods southwest of Kurovitsy, closed in on the positions of the 1st Platoon. At the same time a German observer perched on a high roof reported suspicious movements at the forest's edge due west of the village.

Schneider hardly knew where to turn first. When he arrived at the 2d Platoon's CP, he was informed that a KV tank stood just beyond the mine obstacle on the Vyritsa road and was lobbing shells into Kurovitsy. No other tanks, however, had been observed. Schneider ordered the rocket projectors of the 4th Platoon to assemble at the northern outskirts and prepare to fire in the direction of both the tank and the western approaches to the village.

At 0815 the 5th Platoon took up positions on the western outskirts to defend the village against an attack from that direction. The men arrived in time to see a Russian infantry company moving straight toward them. The Germans opened fire at a range of about 1,000 yards and a lively fight developed. The 1st Platoon was still engaged in warding off the Russian attack from the south when a heavy explosion was heard from the direction of the Vyritsa road. The KV had touched off a mine. Through his glasses Schneider could see the crew climb out of the tank, inspect the damage, and remount. Shortly afterward the KV's gun resumed fire, but the shells went over the roof tops and landed outside the western outskirts of the village.

By 0850 the defense of Kurovitsy had reached a critical stage. The Russian attack from the west was making slow but steady headway against the stubborn resistance of the 5th Platoon. Simultaneously, the fighting in the southern part grew more lively as additional Russian infantry forces came up from the south. The fire from the tank gun became more accurate. During the entire action Schneider's repeated radio messages requesting assistance from the task force commander brought no response.

Schneider thereupon decided to try to reduce the enemy pressure by first silencing the tank gun and then launching a counterattack on the west side. He ordered the rocket projectors to fire a salvo at the tank. Several direct hits were scored, knocking out the tank. However, before the half-tracks had time to turn around and prepare another salvo against the Russian infantry advancing from the west, the range had grown too short for firing rockets. Schneider quickly assembled all the available tanks and half-tracks, led the column 500 yards up the road toward Kobrino, turned off to the left, and drove with all guns ablaze into the flank and rear of the Russian infantry company, which by that time was only some 250 yards from the western outskirts of the town. This thrust caught the Russians by surprise. Most of them were overrun by the tanks, the rest ran for cover or surrendered. The appearance of the German tanks on the west side of the village led the Russian forces attacking from the south to withdraw to the woods north of Staro-Siverskaya. By Q915 the fighting was over and 15 minutes later the advance guard of the 8th Panzer Division's task force entered Kurovitsy from Kobrino.

The task force commander explained to Schneider that his advance had been delayed by a Russian attack from Gatchina during the early morning hours. His force had to assist in the capture of Gatchina before it could jump off on its southward drive. Schneider and his men were ordered to take a well-deserved rest.

During the aforementioned actions the armored engineer company proved effective as an independent combat unit. Excellent teamwork between the tank, rocket projector, and combat engineer platoons made this small unit a formidable fighting force.

The preceding examples are isolated instances in which the Russians were able to delay the German advance during the first months after the invasion of their country. In general, however, the attackers were able to push back the defenders, most of whose armor was destroyed by the combined effort of German antitank guns, artillery, air attacks, and panzer units. The German Army advanced relentlessly to within a short distance of Leningrad and Moscow, forcing the Russians to leave behind even slightly damaged equipment that could have been recovered and repaired. By the winter of 1941-42 the Russians had relatively few tanks to commit. Even so, they never missed an opportunity to counterattack.

THE STRUGGLE FOR SHELTER
(DECEMBER 1941)

The winter of 1941-42 was particularly severe and the fighting on many sectors of the front centered around inhabited localities that could offer shelter from the cold. In mid-December a German patrol captured an operations order that revealed that the Russians planned to attack southwestward along a road leading from the direction of Lisichansk, on the Donets, with the intention of disrupting the German lines of communication. On 18 December the 203d Infantry Regiment moved into a new battle position in and around Berestovaya, a village situated along the expected Russian axis of advance. The regiment organized its center of resistance around the stone buildings in the center of the village (map below).

The 203d had been engaged in heavy defensive fighting for several weeks, and its combat efficiency had dropped sharply. The average strength of the infantry companies had been reduced

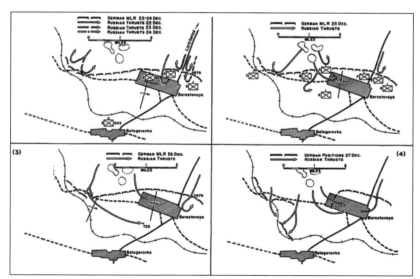

German defense of Berestovaya 22-27 December 1941

to approximately 50 riflemen, and the regiment had lost about one-third of its heavy weapons.

Sprawling villages and a few trees were predominant features of the rolling landscape around Berestovaya, whose stone houses—rare in this part of Russia—provided ample shelter against December temperatures, which averaged about 15° F. The snow cover varied from 4 inches to several feet in depth.

From 18 through 22 December the Russians deployed their forces and pushed back one German outpost after another, an indication that a major attack was imminent. On the evening of 22 December the 2d Battalion was hit by a Russian infantry force of regimental strength. German defensive fire succeeded in stopping the Russian advance on both sides of the Lisichansk-Belogorovka road; however, a German strong point on F Company's left flank was overrun and Russian elements penetrated Berestovaya as far as the 2d Battalion command post. The battalion commander then committed his reserves and restored the situation.

On 23 December the Russians made unsuccessful piecemeal attacks in company to battalion strength against the 2d Battalion sector astride the Lisichansk-Belogorovka road. After darkness had fallen, the Russians fired a brief artillery concentration against the forward positions of G company in the area east of the road; then they attacked the company with 2 battalions of infantry supported by 10 tanks and broke through near Hill 676. German artillery was then brought to bear on the Russian armor, forcing it to withdraw, and the infantry, deprived of tank support, was unable to advance. The Germans thereupon committed Companies I and K of the reserve battalion and sealed off the Russian penetration.

On the 24th the Russians, using only infantry, attacked along the road and, for the first time, against the left flank of the adjacent 1st Battalion.

On Christmas morning the Russians attacked along the road

and eastward with two battalions of infantry, but were stopped by artillery fire. Shortly afterward, two Russian assault groups, each consisting of one to two companies supported by mortar fire, debouched from draws northwest of Berestovaya and attacked A and C Companies. Despite their numerical inferiority, the Germans managed to repulse these attacks.

About 1400, in the face of a sharp east wind, 12 Russian tanks suddenly emerged from the same draws and made a surprise attack toward Berestovaya from the west. Accompanied by infantry, the tanks advanced slowly and brought the German strong points under fire. Within an hour the tanks had broken through Company A's position, where 40 men were trying to hold a 1,000-yard-wide sector. A few of the tanks broke off from their accompanying infantry and moved southward toward the railroad embankment, but withdrew after two tanks had been lost to antitank fire.

Company K counterattacked from the south and cleared the village of those elements that had broken through its defenses. Headquarters Company of the 3d Battalion and I Company were moved up from Belogorovka and committed; by 2100 the German MLR was restored.

The heavy casualties that had been suffered in the action up to that point forced the 203d Infantry Regiment to reorganize the three battalions being assigned adjoining sectors, with the 3d Battalion in the center, flanked by the 1st and 2d on the left and right, respectively. Each battalion held one company in reserve.

At dawn on the 26th the Russians began heavy attacks in the area between Berestovaya and that portion of the rail line due west of the village. Seventeen Russian tanks, accompanied by infantry, moved against the right wing of the 1st Battalion, smashing B Company's position. As the Russians reached the railroad embankment they were halted by German artillery fire. Some of the Russian tanks moved on southeastward toward Hill 728, a conspicuous plateau in the otherwise rolling terrain. The hill offered no cover to the Germans who could not hold it against the Russian tank fire and therefore withdrew southward to the railroad. In order to strengthen the regiment's defenses, division moved one infantry battalion and a squadron of dismounted bicycle infantry to Belogorovka.

German ground-support aircraft were committed during the early morning hours with but little success—the situation on the ground was so confused that accurate bombing and strafing was impossible. At 0930 the Russians penetrated Berestovaya from the west and at noon the regimetal commander gave the 2d Battalion permission to withdraw from the village. However, with the arrival shortly thereafter of reinforcements and five assault guns, the battalion was able to withstand Russian pressure until 1600, when Russian infantry, together with a few tanks, made a fresh attack along the road. The Germans lost two strong points near Hill 676 as the Russians broke through. With the aid of the reserve battalion and the assault guns, the 2d Battalion was able to throw the Russians back. By midnight the 2d Battalion's MLR was restored, but contact had been lost between the 3d and 1st Battalions, the latter having taken up a new defensive position close to the railroad embankment.

At dawn on the 27th the Russians launched an attack fully as powerful as that of the preceding day. Striking from the gap between the 1st and 3d Battalions, a strong infantry force supported by at least 20 tanks attacked the 1st Battalion's positions along the railroad embankment. The battalion's eight 37-mm. antitank guns on the embankment were ineffectual against the Russian T34 tanks and were soon knocked out, whereupon the Germans were forced to give up the embankment.

Toward 1100, after a strong artillery preparation, Russian infantry with tank support attacked from the area just west and northwest of Berestovaya and succeeded in reaching the center of the village. The Germans then counterattacked and recaptured

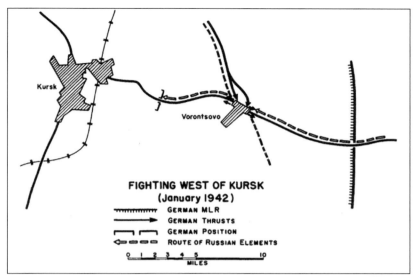

Fighting west of Kursk (January 1942)

it, following which another Russian force enveloped it by sweeping around the south side.

At 1400, a Russian infantry force, accompanied by several tanks, broke into Berestovaya from the west. Shortly afterward a tank-infantry force attacked along the Lisichansk-Belogorovka road and entered the village from the east. The commander of the 2d Battalion then ordered the evacuation of Berestovaya during the night.

The night withdrawal was carried out without interference. The Russians, who had suffered heavy losses, continued to attack the next day, but were so weak that the Germans had no difficulty in stopping any attempt to advance.

This action exemplifies the tenacity with which both parties fought for villages or other permanent-type shelter during the bitter winter of 1941-42. The German defense of Berestovaya was facilitated by the existence of stone houses, which were not as easily destroyed as the usual Russian structures of wood, clay, or straw.

Throughout the course of their repeated attacks the Russians dissipated their offensive strength without forming points of main effort. Tanks were employed exclusively in support of infantry, a characteristic often evident during the first few months of the war. The Russians could have seized Berestovaya with much less effort if they had tried to envelop it from the beginning. An early Russian thrust to the dominating terrain of Hill 728 would have isolated the German forces in and around Berestovaya and made a prolonged defense impossible.

SEESAW BATTLE IN SUBZERO TEMPERATURES (JANUARY 1942)

The beginning ascendancy of Russian armor over its German counterpart is exemplified in the following action, during which the Russian tank units showed themselves more aggressive than usual. In January 1942 the German front near Kursk ran north and south about 20 miles east of the city. Because of heavy snowfall cross-country movements was hampered by deep drifts, and temperatures dropped to $-30°$ F. as sharp winds swept across the rolling countryside.

Since there were no woods in the area, visibility was good, except in low places. The monotony of the landscape was relieved only by a number of villages and towns.

Exposed for the first time to the rigors of a Russian winter, the Germans struggled desperately against the elements, as their tanks, trucks, and automatic weapons broke down in the bitter cold. Timber for the improvement of the positions was scarce; accordingly the exhausted German infantry units, then employed along broad sectors, concentrated their defense in village strong points.

The Russians, taking advantage of their numerical superiority and greater experience under winter conditions, sought to undermine the German defense by a series of local, limited-objective attacks.

In the sector of the German 16th Motorized Infantry Division, Russian reconnaissance patrols had skillfully identified a weak spot at the boundary between two regiments. A combined arms team of Russian armor and infantry succeeded in breaking through the German MLR where it crossed the east-west road leading to Kursk, through which a railway and highway vital to

German supply movements ran parallel to the front.

Exploiting the breakthrough, a force of about 25 T34 tanks with infantry mounted on them drove on toward Kursk and easily captured the communities in its path which were held solely by German service units. The Russian thrust continued into the next day, when it was stopped about 5 miles from Kursk by a hastily assembled German force. Several attempts to close the gap in the MLR with weak local reserves failed, and the Russians were able to follow up their tank force with two or three battalions of infantry, including some mounted in trucks.

The town of Vorontsovo, situated on the road leading to Kursk, was occupied by a weak Russian force. A German tank battalion, whose tank strength had fallen to 22, was released from another sector and sent in from the north against the right flank of the breakthrough force. The battalion took Vorontsovo by a coup de main, whereupon the Russians had to discontinue their westward advance.

After receiving meager reinforcements in the form of one 88-mm. antiaircraft gun and a battalion of infantry replacements that had just arrived from the zone of interior, the Germans conducted harassing raids in the areas east and west of Vorontsovo, effectively interfering with the supply of those Russian troops that had been cutoff west of the town. On the third day of the action these isolated Russian forces attacked with infantry and tanks but were repulsed.

On the following day, during a driving snowstorm, the Russians attacked Vorontsovo from both the east and west, the thrust from the west being supported by tanks. Taking advantage of their greater ground clearance and lower ground pressure, the Russian tanks swept across terrain that the Germans had considered impassable for armor.

The young German infantry replacements, untested in battle, lacked experience in hand-to-hand fighting in villages and towns. They had not yet learned to fight in conjunction with tanks and were quickly overcome. Inferior in fire power and mobility to their Russian opposites, the German tanks were almost completely wiped out, and Vorontsovo was once again in Russian hands.

The Russian attack on this key town from two opposite directions was perfectly coordinated. The Germans never found out whether the two Russian forces had established radio contact or whether, perhaps, they were assisted by civilians who had remained in the town. Executed in a driving snowstorm, the Russian attack achieved surprise because the German precautions were inadequate. Extensive reconnaissance and security measures are elementary precautions that must be taken, regardless of the weather. To be derelict in these essentials is to risk lives.

The German counterattack was inadequately supported and led, and the inexperienced infantry were more a hindrance than a help in the operation. An armored unit on an independent mission must be accompanied by seasoned troops equipped with the necessary supporting weapons.

THE FEDORENKO ORDER
(JUNE 1942)

The Russians realized the superiority of the T34 tank early in the war and converted their plant facilities to the sole production of this one model. During their first winter in Russia the Germans encountered enemy tanks either singly or in small groups. This scarcity of armor came about because the production of new tanks was low and because many of those which did become available were used far behind the front to train crews on the latest tactical doctrine. With the improvement in optical and radio equipment, the Russian command was finally able to organize large armored formations and employ them in far-reaching operations.

Although the Russian military had reason to be satisfied with the local successes achieved during the winter of 1941-42, it was nevertheless fully aware of the deficiencies still inherent in the tactics of large armored formations. It thus felt obliged to intervene in armored affairs at the end of June 1942, and did so by issuing a new directive, which was particularly important because its author, Fedorenko (Chief Marshal of Tanks and Mechanized Forces and Deputy Commander of Defense), drew the right inference from previous mistakes.

That these conclusions were correct was proved by subsequent developments. It is to be assumed that the basic principles expressed in this order continue to govern the employment of Russian armor to this very day. The following is a translation of the Fedorenko Order:

SUBJECT: Employment of Armored Formations

TO: All Armored Forces Commanders at Front Headquarters and Army Headquarters, and Commanding Generals of Armored Armies and Corps.

Testing the T-34's capabilities with petrol bombs.

An analysis of the combat operations of several armored corps in May 1942 indicates that commanders of armored forces at front headquarters [Ed: Russian equivalent of an army group, subsequently referred to as such] and at army headquarters lack comprehension of the basic principles governing the employment of major armored formations in modern warfare. The XII Armored Corps, for instance, committed on the right of a force attacking in the direction of Kharkov, was split up into single brigades and employed piecemeal, with the result that the commander of armored forces at the superior army group headquarters was unable to conduct the operations of the corps. The XXI and XXII Armored Corps on the left of the attack force were identified by the enemy long before their commitment in battle. Once again, the commander of armored forces at army group headquarters had no control whatsoever over his subordinate corps.

Until the official regulations for the employment of armored troops are approved and issued by the People's Commissar for Defense, the following orders will be observed:

1. The armored corps is a basic unit and will be reserved for the execution of strategic missions.

2. The armored corps is subordinate to the army group headquarters and will be committed for the execution of strategic missions in conjunction with other troop formations of the army group.

3. It is forbidden to place armored corps under the command of armies and to split them up for the purpose of reinforcing the infantry. An armored corps committed within the area of an army will operate in conjunction with that army for the duration of a designated operation, while simultaneously maintain ing contact with army group headquarters.

4. In an offensive operation conducted by an army group, an armored corps has the mission of massing its forces for a deep thrust, enveloping the enemy's main forces, encircling them, and destroying them in co-operation with the air force and with other ground units.

5. In order to preserve the striking power of an armored corps for a strategic envelopment and the ensuing struggle deep in the enemy's rear, it is forbidden to employ armored corps for breaking through fortified positions. However, when reinforced by artillery, tactical air force, infantry, and engineers, an armored corps may be committed for a frontal breakthrough attempt against prepared enemy positions.

6. An armored corps may drive ahead of the other friendly forces and penetrate the enemy sector to a depth of 25 to 30 miles, provided that a second wave is sent through the gap. The situation will often require that, immediately after a breakthrough of the hostile positions, the enemy's main forces—located 10 to 15 miles behind the MLR—are enveloped, encircled, and annihilated with the assistance of other formations.

7. The armored corps is considered to be capable of 72-96 hours of uninterrupted commitment.

8. The accomplishment of an armored corps' mission depends essentially upon the training and esprit de corps of its

personnel, on air support, and on proper coordination with the artillery, tactical air force units, engineers, and other arms and services.

9. Once it has achieved a strategic envelopment, an armored corps will establish contact with airlanded troops and partisan units.

10. During defensive operations an armored corps will be committed in counterattacks against any enemy forces that have broken through the friendly MLB or have enveloped the flanks, especially if these forces consist of armored and motorized units. In such instances the counterthrust will not be executed as a frontal maneuver, but will be delivered against the enemy's flank or rear.

11. In any event, surprise is of the essence in committing an armored corps. For this reason the assembly or regrouping of forces will always be carried out by night. Should a regrouping during the day become inevitable, it will be carried out in groups of no more than three to five tanks.

12. Terrain factors must be given foremost consideration in selecting the direction for an armored corps attack. They must be favorable for the mass commitment of armor.

13. If intact rail facilities are available, the cross-country movement of tanks over distances exceeding 30 miles is forbidden.

14. In planning the commitment of an armored corps, especially in a strategic envelopment, adequate supplies of fuel, ammunition, rations, and spare parts must be prepared for the entire duration of the operation, and the tank recovery service must be appropriately organized. The following quantities of supply will normally be carried by the combat trains:

  • Fuel—Equivalent of three times the vehicle's capacity.
  • Ammunition—Two to three basic issues.
  • Rations—Five daily.

The tank crews will carry the following additional rations: two to three tins of canned meat or hard sausage, canned ham, soup concentrates in cubes, bread, zwieback, sugar, and tea or water in vacuum bottles .

15. The armored corps commanders and the armored forces commanders, as well as the military council of the army group, will be held responsible for the proper employment of the armored corps in combat as well as for their logistical and technical support.

The effect of the Fedorenko Order was not immediately noticeable. In the summer of 1942 the Germans once more seized the initiative on most sectors of the Russian front. The Russians, still handicapped by a shortage of up-to-date tanks, were forced to use their slower and less maneuverable heavies in conjunction with the T34's. They resorted to a number of ruses and ambushes in an effort to gain a maximum of time at the loss of a minimum of space. Backed by a steadily mounting tank production, they made every effort to ward off the German onslaught by skillful defensive maneuvers.

FEINT, AMBUSH, AND STRIKE (JULY 1942)

The following actions took place in July 1942 on the central front during an attack by two panzer divisions supported by two infantry divisions. The Russians held well-fortified positions protected by extensive mine fields. At some points the Russian defensive system reached a depth of 3 miles. The German objective was to thrust toward the Resseta River, in the vicinity of which additional Russian fortifications were under construction. Aerial photographs taken before the attack was launched did not reveal the presence of any Russian tanks.

During the first 2 days the attack proceeded according to plan. The two infantry divisions crossed the mine belt and fought their way through the Russian positions. On the third day the two panzer divisions were moved up and committed in the direction of the Resseta. The 11th Panzer Division was at full strength, whereas the 19th had only 60 percent of its prescribed T/O & E. Only about half the armored infantry units were motorized, the others had to march on foot. The Russians, meanwhile, had moved up reinforcements, including tanks. Their air forces, particularly the fighter-bomber squadrons, were quite active.

The fighting took place in or near very dense forests, where visibility was poor. The watercourses could be forded at several points. The weather was warm and sunny.

When the 19th Panzer Division attacked northeastward from Kholmishchi, the forward armored elements ran into strong Russian antitank defenses south of Nikitskoye (map overleaf). In devising their defense system, the Russians had taken full advantage of the concealment offered by the terrain and vegetation. One German armored column drove straight into an antitank gun front disposed on a semicircle facing south. The

 contains the following labels:

Ressela R.

Dretovo
Polyana
Kolosovo
Glinnaya

Vytebet R.

Nikitskoye

Rechitsa

XX
19

XX
11

Kholmishchi

Ulyanovo

Bryansk

**GERMAN ADVANCE TO THE RESSETA RIVER
(July 1942)**

→ GERMAN AXIS OF ADVANCE

0 1 2 3 4 5   10
MILES

German advance to the Resseta River (July 1942)

Russian guns, emplaced in pairs for mutual support, were dug in so that the muzzles were just above the surface of the ground. Between each pair of guns was an additional antitank gun mounted on a two-wheeled farm cart. The cart-mounted guns were camouflaged, but no effort had been made to conceal them.

As the German tanks advanced, the dug-in guns fired a volley, then ceased. Seeking the source of the fire, the Germans noticed the guns mounted on carts, and moved toward the newly discovered targets. As soon as a German tank turned to bring the cart-mounted guns under fire, it was hit from the side by Russian antitank fire from the concealed positions. The cart-mounted guns were dummies. Several of the tanks were lost in the action before the Germans succeeded in knocking out all the real antitank guns. In emplaning the dummy guns, the Russians were careful to leave just enough of the gun visible to make it an attractive target. Taken in by this ruse, the Germans turned their tanks to face the decoys, thereby exposing tracks and lateral armor, the most vulnerable parts.

After elements of the 19th Panzer Division had pushed through Nikitskoye they ran into trouble north of the town, where they were repeatedly attacked by groups of five to seven Russian tanks emerging from the large forest adjacent to the division's left flank. After allowing the German armored point to pass, the Russian tanks pounced upon the wheeled vehicles which followed. Whenever the Germans counterattacked, the Russian tanks immediately withdrew into the forest, only to emerge at another point. The tanks used in this operation were of an older type, no match for their German counterparts in open terrain. Hence the Russians used them—and with telling effect— only for hit-and-run operations. These Russian tactics cost the Germans a large number of casualties and caused considerable delay.

The German division commander thereupon ordered one tank battalion to cover the left flank of the advancing column. Echeloned in depth and supported by armored engineers, the tanks proceeded to comb the edge of the forest. In this manner the column was protected against any further surprise attacks.

When committing tanks in densely wooded areas, the Germans found it expedient to have them accompanied by infantry or engineers because the tank crews were unable to see or hear enough to proceed safely on their own.

Meanwhile, the 11th Panzer Division, driving toward the Resseta on the right of the 19th, attacked northeastward from Ulyanovo according to plan. As the leading tanks approached the village of Rechitsa, several T34's suddenly debouched from deep gullies and attacked the German armor from the left flank. After a stiff fight the T34's disappeared into the gullies only to renew their attacks at another point farther north.

The German medium tanks sent in pursuit were suddenly hit by flanking fire delivered from nearby gullies. In seeking the source of this fire the Germans observed that the Russians had dug in heavy tanks in such a way that only the turrets and guns were visible. The Russian heavies held their fire until the German tanks were within range or, when bypassed by the Germans, rolled backward out of the gullies and raced northward.

Although the Russian tanks were outnumbered, their tactics, well suited to the terrain, took a heavy toll of German armor. The Russians skillfully exploited the superior fire power of their heavy tanks and the maneuverability of their T34's in a way that compensated for the slowness of the former and the shortage of the latter.

At first the 11th Panzer Division commander tried to cope with these unusual tactics by committing artillery and antitank guns. When these proved ineffective, he asked for air support. Reconnaissance planes, protected by fighters, hovered over the area, maintaining constant radio contact with division headquarters. At least one reconnaissance plane circled at all times above the division's axis of advance and reported the hideouts of the Russian tanks by radio or flares. This information was relayed to the German tank commanders. As a result of good air-ground teamwork, the Russian armor was driven back after suffering heavy losses.

Despite the initial setback, this armored action was brought to a rapid and successful conclusion. Once the reconnaissance planes had established the presence of Russian armor, they kept the hostile tanks under observation until the latter were annihilated by their German counterparts or were withdrawn toward the north.

But the 11th Panzer Division had not seen the last of the elusive T34's. As the division attacked Kolosovo, its last objective before reaching the Resseta, the Russians dispatched twenty T34's from the direction of Dretovo, less than a mile from the river.

As soon as they established contact with the advancing elements of the German armor just north of Kolosovo, the T34's began to withdraw, fighting a delaying action. After the German tank formations had all passed through Kolosovo, they were brought under heavy antitank fire from the woods north of the town. Most of the German armor then swung to the left, toward the forest, while the remainder held to the main axis of advance. As the German tanks that had veered off were approaching the immediate vicinity of the forest, an entire brigade of T34's broke out of Polyana, west of Kolosovo, and hit the German tanks from the flank and rear, forcing them to withdraw to Kolosovo, which changed hands several times during the bitter tank battle that ensued. Only after the German division commander had thrown in all his artillery and antitank guns were the Germans able to obtain a firm hold on the town.

The advance and subsequent withdrawal of the twenty T34's slowed the German northward advance, setting up a perfect target for the antitank guns north of Kolosovo. This antitank-gun ambush, insufficient in itself to hurt the German division seriously, diverted the attention of the Germans while the Russian tank brigade struck a punishing blow against the German flank and rear. The three phases of the Russian tactical plan—the feint, the ambush, and the strike of the tank brigade— were perfectly coordinated. On the other hand, if the German air and ground reconnaissance had operated effectively, the panzer division commander would have been warned of the Russian intentions in time.

During the actions which took place south of the Resseta River, the Russians revealed their skill in adapting armored tactics to different types of terrain. Despite numerical inferiority they were able to inflict severe losses and delay the German advance.

In contrast to the engagements that were fought during the winter of 1941-42, Russian tanks appeared in brigade formation in the early months of 1942. The majority of these newly formed units were composed of T34's, occasionally interspersed with a few light tanks and some 52-ton KV's. The armored brigades had no organic infantry, artillery, or antitank units. In most instances they were employed to penetrate the German MLR, to widen the gap, and to achieve a breakthrough in depth. Rifle brigades or divisions were usually coupled with the armored brigades, either during the first phase of the attack—when the infantrymen rode into battle mounted on tanks—or after a penetration had been achieved to widen the gap and secure the flanks. For the latter purpose the Russians employed both foot and motorized infantry. Even on foot Russian infantrymen often kept pace with the advancing armor and proved capable of consolidating and holding the territory gained by the tanks.

AMBUSH WITHOUT FOLLOWUP
(DECEMBER 1942)

In December 1942, when the Germans were putting up a desperate struggle in the Stalingrad pocket, their drive into the Caucasus had been stopped about 300 miles from the Baku oil fields. The German 3d Panzer Division was in the area northeast of Mozdok covering the left flank of the First Panzer Army, which had gone over to the defensive. In front of the division's right wing a continuous line of defense had been formed which dwindled to a mere security line as it ran northward toward the division boundary (map below). The Russian forces north of the Terek River were steadily receiving reinforcements and their reconnaissance patrols constantly probed the weaker sectors of the division front. Between the division and Stalingrad, 250 miles to the north, there was only a

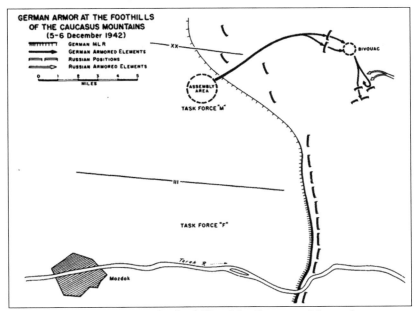

German armor at the foothills of the Caucasus Mountains
(5-6 December 1942)

German armored infantry division and "Group Velmy," a motley unit composed of non-German volunteers.

The steppe in this area was devoid of vegetation and habitation, the monotony of the desertlike terrain being relieved only by small hills.

At noon on 4 December the division was ordered to attack the Russian forces to its left while continuing to provide flank protection for the army's left. The attack was set for the next day.

Carrying out simultaneous holding and attack operations presented a serious problem, in that the division was understrength and had sufficient gasoline for an operational radius of only 100 miles.

The division commander divided his forces into two groups: Task Force M was to mount the attack and Task Force F was to hold. The attack force, under one of the regimental commanders, comprised two tank companies, one infantry company mounted in armored personnel carriers, two armored reconnaissance platoons, and one battery of self-propelled 105-mm. howitzers.

On 5 December Task Force M moved out. After a slow march of about 7 miles over difficult terrain, it encountered stiff resistance from dug-in Russian infantry. About 3 hours later the Russian defenses were finally overcome, but further movement that day was rendered impractical by the approach of darkness. Just before nightfall German air reconnaissance reported Russians in unknown strength about 3 miles southeast of the site selected for the bivouac. To the east and northeast, however, no enemy forces were reported.

Early on the morning of the 6th the task force fanned out in two columns toward the reported enemy concentration. The tank companies formed the left column; the armored infantry company, somewhat weakened by the previous day's engagement, the right. Some infantrymen were assigned to protect the artillery battery that covered the advance.

After an advance of about 1 mile the German columns ran

into Russian infantry, which was well supported by mortars and antitank guns. As the Russian infantry engaged the task force frontally, 15 Russian tanks suddenly emerged from a hollow and fired point blank on the flank of the German left column. One of the two German tank company commanders was killed and two tanks were knocked out. It was only by virtue of the fact that the Russians did not attempt to pursue their advantage that the task force was able to disengage.

Here was an instance where the Russians skillfully withheld their tanks until the German armor was pinned down by frontal fire. The task force was not strong enough to be deployed in depth. Had it been, an attack could have been mounted against the Russian flank.

The Germans failed to perform ground reconnaissance and to secure their flanks during the advance.

RUSSIAN RECONNAISSANCE IN FORCE BY TANK-MOUNTED INFANTRY (OCTOBER 1943)

Early in October 1943, the German 196th Infantry Regiment occupied defensive positions within a forest about 20 miles north of Kiev. Although both flanks were well protected, the positions themselves were vulnerable because the soil was loose and sandy. The Germans neglected to plant antipersonnel mines but did lay antitank mines across roads leading toward their main line of resistance. Behind the MLR they erected roadblocks, covered by dug-in 50-mm. antitank guns.

The ground sloped gently upward in the direction of the Russian MLR, which was then located along the crest of a flat ridge about 2,000 yards north of the German MLR (map opposite).

On 5 October the Russians made the first of a series of forward moves. These movements remained undetected until German observers discovered that the ground had been broken in the vicinity of Advance Position A. Later in the day Russian artillery fired smoke shells on such known German targets as the forester's house and the road intersections. German artillery and mortar fire against the Russian forward positions was ineffective. The patrols that probed the enemy during the night were repulsed.

During the following 2 days the Russians moved their positions forward over 500 yards to Position B. Again the movements remained unobserved because the intermittent rain restricted visibility. Heavy German mortar fire succeeded only in drawing more violent Russian mortar and artillery fire on the road intersections near the fringes of the forest. As German night

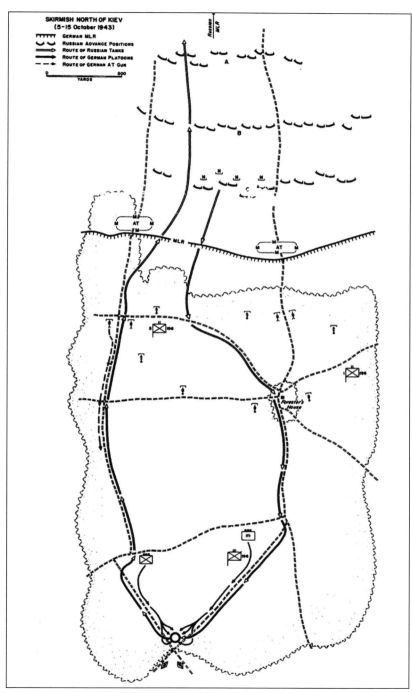

Skirmish north of Kiev (5-15 October 1943)

patrols probed forward, they began to encounter Russian patrols in increasing numbers.

By 10 October the Russians had succeeded in establishing themselves along Advance Position C, only 500 yards from the German MLR. Under the protective cover of mortar and artillery fire, reinforced German reconnaissance patrols were sent out during the day to determine the strength and disposition of the Russian forces and positions and to occupy the latter, should they be found deserted. However, after advancing scarcely 100 yards the patrols came under such heavy mortar fire that they were forced to turn back with heavy casualties.

When the weather cleared, the Germans were able to observe all three Russian advance positions, but could not spot any further movement. During the night the Russian positions were placed under harassing mortar and infantry weapon fire. While three German patrols were being driven off in front of Position C, numerous Russian reconnaissance parties infiltrated the intermediate area and at some points approached to within a few yards of the German main line of resistance.

For the next three nights the Russians were busy digging in along Advance Position C. Heavy rains helped to dampen the noises of their intrenching activities. Shortly after dusk on 12 October, a German patrol finally succeeded in reaching the fringes of Position C. After having spotted some hasty intrenchments, all of which appeared deserted, the Germans were driven back to their lines by three Russian patrols which, supported by nine light machineguns, suddenly appeared from nowhere.

Heavy rains fell again in the evening of 13 October. At 2300 the Russians began to rake the entire German sector with a savage artillery barrage which lasted two hours. Over the din of the exploding shells the sound of approaching tanks could be distinguished in the German forward area. However, the tank noise soon faded away, giving every indication that the armor had been withdrawn.

Toward noon of the next day, in a driving rain, a 3-man German patrol succeeded in crawling into the forward Russian positions. They were still deserted and gave the appearance of having been occupied for only a very short time. The Germans concluded at once that these were dummy positions. Unknown to the members of the patrol at the time was the fact that they had been closely observed by the Russians, who nevertheless permitted them to reconnoiter the positions unmolested, feeling certain that their true intentions would not be revealed.

Meanwhile, the Russians were proceeding with preparations for their reconnaissance mission inside the German lines.

During the afternoon of 14 October, a 20-man patrol, including an officer and two noncommissioned officers, was selected from a Russian rifle company which had been resting in a village behind the lines. These men were all specially selected, veteran fighters familiar with the terrain since all of them had originally come from the Kiev region. Each man was provided with 2 days' rations, 1 1/2 days' ammunition supply, and 6 hand grenades. The officer was issued a two-way radio. He and his noncommissioned officers carried submachineguns while the rest of the men were armed with automatic rifles. After reaching a trench in the vicinity of Position A, the patrol was met by a Russian officer who briefed them as follows:

You will move out and proceed to Advance Position C where you will join four tanks that have been dug in. Tomorrow you are to mount the tanks, advance on the German positions facing us, penetrate them, and drive into the wooded enemy rear area. Nothing should be allowed to delay your forward progress since everything depends on lightning speed. Knock down whatever gets in your way but avoid any prolonged encounter. Remember your primary mission is to gain information about German positions, how they are manned, and where the enemy artillery, mortars, and obstacles are emplaced. Don't stop to take prisoners until your return trip; one or two will suffice. You must create fear and terror behind the enemy lines and then withdraw as swiftly as you came.

Late that same evening the patrol moved out toward the German lines. Despite enemy harassing fire it reached the tanks in Position C at 0100. The tanks, with their crews inside, had been dug in by engineers and were well camouflaged. The entrances to the pits sloped upward toward the rear.

The infantry patrol was now split into squads of five men and each squad was assigned to a tank. The men were ordered to dig in close to their tanks, maintain absolute silence, and remain covered, especially after daybreak.

At dawn all was quiet and well concealed. A light haze hovered over the area in the early morning hours and toward afternoon turned into fog, limiting visibility to about 300 yards. At approximately 1600 an officer suddenly came up from the direction of the Russian MLR and ordered the patrol to mount at once. The engines were quickly started and, as the camouflage nets were removed, the infantrymen jumped on their respective tanks. Within a matter of minutes the tanks backed out of their pits, formed a single column to the front, and raced toward the German line at top speed. After the tanks had overrun several trenches, the first German soldiers could be seen. However, none of them made any attempt to fire but scrambled for cover at the unexpected sight of the tanks.

Having penetrated the center of the German MLR the tanks moved cross-country through heavy underbrush before taking to the road. As they neared the forester's house, a German water detail was spotted running for cover in great haste. The tanks upset two ration trucks that were blocking the road and sped deep into the German lines. About 1,000 yards beyond the forester's house the Russians suddenly turned half-right and followed the road leading into the woods. After proceeding

Russian T-34 in action.

another 1,000 yards they approached a crossroad and decided to stop. Enjoying a commanding view of the road intersection, the Russians dismounted and prepared all-around defenses right in the midst of the German positions, hardly 700 yards away from the regimental CP. The tanks formed the core of the position; the infantrymen dug in around the cluster of armor. The Russian officer quickly established radio contact with his lines and exchanged messages.

Before long German infantry assault and combat engineer platoons, equipped with close-combat antitank weapons, moved, in from two directions and surrounded the Russians. However, they could approach no closer than 150 yards from the tanks because the sparsely wooded forest afforded the Russians excellent observation and permitted them to fire at everything that moved. Finding themselves pinned down, the Germans sent a detail to the left flank of their MLR for one of the 50-mm. antitank guns. Since the static gun was dug in and had to be pulled by hand, its arrival would be delayed. Finally, at 1800, two self-propelled assault guns from division moved into position to the south of the tanks, opened fire, and wounded a number of Russian riflemen.

Leaving their wounded behind, the Russians within 10 minutes mounted their tanks and sped off in a northerly direction toward their own lines with tank guns blazing in all directions.

Darkness was setting in when the 50-mm. antitank gun detail spotted the approaching Russian tanks. The German crew had no opportunity to fire their piece and barely succeeded in getting off the road. They remained under cover until the last Russian tank had passed. After quickly pulling their gun into position the Germans fired at the rear tank and scored a direct hit, killing two of the mounted infantrymen.

When it had become quite dark the Russian lead tank turned its headlights on and, with the other three tanks following closely behind, sped unmolested across the German main line of resistance. After they reached open terrain the Russians dimmed the lights and raced northward into the night in the direction of their positions.

This was a daring Russian undertaking, meticulously prepared and executed with boldness and speed. However, it was clowned with success primarily because of the inadequacy of the German antitank defenses. The Russians must have been aware of the sparse minefields and the shortage of self-propelled antitank guns.

The Russians spent a great deal of time on preparations by allowing themselves an interval of several days between their advances from Position A to B and from B to C. Then there was still another interval of several days before the tanks moved into position; finally, two more days elapsed before the action was actually launched.

The Russians were extremely adept in carrying out and concealing large-scale intrenching activities, such as the digging of tank pits.

In making their positions appear totally deserted during the daytime and by creating dummy positions which patrols were purposely induced to reconnoiter, the Germans, if not completely misled, were at least left in doubt as to the true Russian intentions.

Still another safeguard that the Russians used again and again to insure maximum surprise was to move up their infantry at the latest possible moment, usually not until the night preceding an operation. In this manner they eliminated the possibility of capture by enemy patrols and the potential disclosure of their plans.

Three weeks after the action just described, the Germans discovered how skillfully the Russians had camouflaged the approach movements of their tanks. A Russian prisoner told of how the tanks were moved forward, masked by the noise of the artillery barrage. Since this concealment was not fully adequate they went a step further. By initially sending six tanks and then immediately withdrawing two the Russians strove to create the impression that all tanks had been pulled back. This ruse was employed with complete success.

That the Russians decided to stop at the road crossing seemed a blunder. The ensuing loss of time might well have led to the annihilation of the patrol had the Germans employed their assault guns from the north rather than from the south and had they been able to block the roads leading northward to the MLR with mines and antitank guns. Why the Russians suddenly stopped and dug in is not specifically explained. The stop, however, did permit them to establish radio contact. It is therefore reasonable to assume that in this instance, as in so many others, the Russian lower echelon command lacked the imagination and initiative necessary to continue the action beyond its immediate scope.

TANKS FAIL TO ELIMINATE A BRIDGEHEAD (JUNE 1944)

This action, which occurred in 1944, shows that the principles laid down by Fedorenko had taken root and were being put into practice. It was symptomatic of the progressive improvement in Russian methods of employing armor.

At the end of May 1944, following a series of retrograde movements, the German front in the Kishinev area ran along the west bank of the Dnestr River. The characteristic terrain features in that area are the low hills and patches of forest. The east bank of the Dnestr overlooked German defenses (map opposite).

Anticipating an early resumption of the Russian offensive, the German corps commander organized a task force of 40 tanks and armored infantry with personnel carriers and held it in reserve at a centrally located point about 10 miles from the river. Assembly areas for a counterattack and approach routes to the river line were carefully reconnoitered and extra fuel was loaded onto all vehicles.

At 2200 on 1 June the Russians attacked in force across the river and quickly established a bridgehead 3 to 5 miles deep and about 7 miles wide. The German task force was immediately alerted to counterattack at dawn in conjunction with the infantry that had been pushed back from the river line.

The German counterblow began with an artillery preparation. At first the tanks encountered heavy fire from Russian antitank guns, but, once these were neutralized, the German counterattack made good progress, and the Russian infantry was routed from its unfinished field fortifications along the bridgehead perimeter.

The task force did not encounter any tanks within the bridgehead because the Russians had not had opportunity to put them across the river. However, as soon as the Russian tank

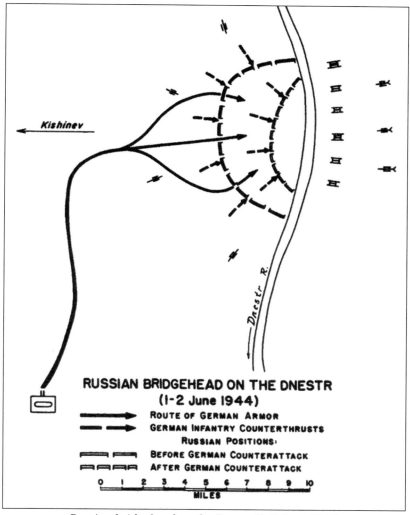

Russian bridgehead on the Dnestr (1-2 June 1944)

commander was informed of the German counterattack, he moved his armor out of the staging area where it had been awaiting the signal to cross. The tanks then drove onto the higher ground overlooking the river and supported the Russian artillery that was deployed along the bank. While the artillery fired on the advancing German infantry, the tanks were employed as roving antitank guns in the absence of tank destroyers.

Without the protection of a dense smoke screen and strong

artillery and fighter-bomber support, the German task force was unable to eliminate the bridgehead. No chemical ammunition was available, and the ground-support aircraft, even though it did knock out a few Russian tanks at the beginning of the engagement, had to withdraw soon afterward when Russian antiaircraft fire over the bridgehead area grew more intensive. The German counterattack finally bogged down about 2,500 yards short of the river bank, having reduced but not eliminated the Russian bridgehead.

Had the counterattack taken place before daylight, the German task force might have reached its objective. This could only have been achieved by launching a night attack immediately after the first enemy crossings, while most of the Russian forces were still astride the river. Although the task force was assembled only 10 miles from the river, it had to drive 19 miles over winding roads to reach the crossing site. In an ideal situation the task force would have been just far enough from the river to be out of effective artillery range, and yet near enough to be within immediate striking distance of any potential landing site. It should be pointed out, however, that by 1944 tanks were so scarce in the German Army that relatively small armored units had to act as reserves along overextended frontages. In this instance shortages forced the Germans to abandon established tactical principles and, as a result, they suffered the consequences.

AN ARMORED TASK FORCE
SEIZES TWO VITAL BRIDGES
(AUGUST 1944)

In those isolated instances in which German armored units were at full strength, they were still able to attain local successes, even in the summer of 1944. During the nights of 13 and 14 August 1944 the 3d Panzer Division detrained at Kielce in southern Poland. The division's mission was to stop the advance of Russian forces that had broken through the German lines during the collapse of Army Group Center and to assist the withdrawing German formations in building up a new defense line near the upper Vistula.

In order to allow all units of his division the time needed to prepare for their next commitment and at the same time secure his route of advance, the division commander decided to form an armored task force from the units that had detrained first. The force was to be led by the commander of the 2d Tank Battalion and was to consist of Tank Companies E and F, equipped with Panther tanks, one armored infantry company mounted in armored personnel carriers, and one battery equipped with self-propelled 105-mm. howitzers. The task force was to launch a surprise attack on Village Z, situated approximately 30 miles east of Kielce, and seize the bridges south and east of the village in order to permit the main body of the division to advance along the Kielce-Opatow road toward the Vistula (map overleaf).

The attack was to be launched at dawn on 16 August. According to air reconnaissance information obtained at 1800 on 15 August, Village Z was held by relatively weak Russian forces and no major troop movements were observed in the area. The only German unit stationed in the area between Kielce and Village Z was the 188th Infantry Regiment, which occupied the

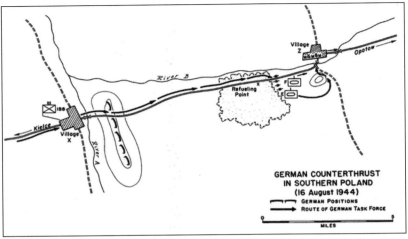

German counterthrust in southern Poland (16 August 1944)

high ground east of River A and whose command post was in Village X.

The terrain was hilly. Fields planted with grain, potatoes, and beets were interspersed with patches of forest. The weather was sunny and dry, with high daytime temperatures and cool moonlit nights. The hours of sunrise and sunset were 0445 and 1930, respectively.

The task force commander received his orders at 2000 on 15 August and immediately began to study the plan of attack. Since the units that were to participate in the operation had not yet been alerted, the entire task force could not possibly be ready to move out before 2300. The maximum speed at which his force could drive over a dusty dirt road without headlights was 6 miles an hour. The approach march to Village Z would therefore require a minimum of 5 hours. Taking into account the time needed for refueling and deploying his units, the commander arrived at the conclusion that the attack could not be launched before dawn. Since the operation might thus be deprived of the element of surprise, he decided to employ an advance guard that was to move out one hour earlier than the bulk of his force, reach Village X by 0200 at the latest, and cover the remaining 9 miles in 1 1/2 hours. After a short halt the advance guard could launch the attack on Village Z just before dawn.

At 2020 the task force commander assembled the commanders of the participating units at his CP and issued the following verbal orders:

Company F, 6th Tank Regiment, reinforced by one platoon of armored infantry, will form an advance guard that will be ready to move out at 2200 in order to seize Village Z and the two bridges across River B by a coup de main. A reconnaissance detachment will guide the advance guard to Village X. Two trucks loaded with gasoline will be taken along for refueling, which is scheduled to take place in the woods two miles west of Village Z.

The main body of the task force will follow the advance guard at 2300 and form a march column in the following order: 2d Tank Battalion Headquarters, Company E of the 6th Tank Regiment, Battery A of the 75th Artillery Regiment, and Company A of the 3d Armored Infantry Regiment (less one platoon). After crossing River A, the tank company will take the lead, followed by battalion headquarters, the armored infantry company, and the artillery battery in that order.

The task force will halt and refuel in the woods 2 miles west of Village Z. Radio silence will be lifted after River A has been crossed.

The commander of Company F will leave at 2100 and accompany me to the CP of the 188th Infantry Regiment and establish contact with that unit. Company E's commander will take charge of the march column from Kielce to Village X.

Upon receiving these instructions the commander of Company F, Lieutenant Zobel, returned to his unit, assembled the platoon leaders, the first sergeant, and the maintenance section chief and briefed them. He indicated the march route, which they entered on their maps. For the march from Kielce to Village X, the headquarters section was to drive at the head of the column, followed by the four tank platoons, the armored infantry platoon, the gasoline trucks, and the mess and maintenance sections. The ranking platoon leader was to be in charge of the column until Zobel joined it in Village X. Hot coffee was to be served half an hour before the time of departure, which was scheduled for 2200. The reconnaissance detachment was to move out at 2130 and post guides along the road to Village X.

After issuing these instructions to his subordinates, Zobel rejoined the task force commander, with whom he drove to Village X. When they arrived at the CP of the 188th Infantry Regiment, they were given detailed information on the situation. They learned that, after heavy fighting in the Opatow region, the regiment had withdrawn to its present positions during the night of 14-15 August. Attempts to establish a continuous line in conjunction with other units withdrawing westward from the upper Vistula were under way. The Russians had so far not advanced beyond Village Z. Two Polish civilians who had been seized in the woods west of the village had stated that no Russians were to be seen in that forest.

The task force commander thereupon ordered Zobel to carry out the plan of attack as instructed. Zobel awaited the arrival of the advance guard at the western outskirts of Village X. When the column pulled in at 0145, Zobel assumed command and re-formed the march column with the 1st Tank Platoon in the lead, followed by the headquarters section, the 2d and 3d Tank Platoons, the armored infantry platoon, the wheeled elements, and the 4th Tank Platoon.

A guide from the 188th Infantry Regiment rode on the lead tank of the 1st Platoon until it reached the outpost area beyond River A. The column arrived at the German outpost at 0230. The sentry reported that he had not observed any Russian movements during the night. Zobel radioed the task force commander that he was going into action.

To permit better observation the tanks drove with open hatches. The tank commanders stood erect with their heads emerging from the cupolas, listening with a headset. The other apertures of the tanks were buttoned up. Gunners and loaders stood by to open fire at a moment's notice. In anticipation of an encounter with Russian tanks the guns were loaded with armor-piercing shells.

At 0345 the advance guard reached the wooded area in which it was to halt and refuel. The tanks formed two rows, one on each side of the road, while armored infantrymen provided security to the east and west of the halted column. Sentries were posted at 50-yard intervals in the forest north and south of the road. Trucks loaded with gasoline cans drove along the road between the two rows of tanks, stopping at each pair of tanks to unload the full cans and picking up the empties on their return trip. The loaders helped the drivers to refuel and check their vehicles. The gunners checked their weapons, while each radio operator drew coffee for his tank crew. Zobel gave the platoon leaders and tank commanders a last briefing and asked one of the returning truck drivers to hand-carry a message on the progress of the operation to the task force commander in Village X.

According to Zobel's plan of assault, the advance guard was to emerge from the woods in two columns. The one on the left was to comprise the 1st Tank Platoon, headquarters section, and the 4th Tank Platoon, whereas the right column was to be composed of the 2d and 3d Tank Platoons and the armored infantry platoon. The 1st Platoon was to take up positions opposite the southern edge of Village Z, the 2d at the foot of the hill to the south of it. Under the protection of these two platoons the 3d and 4th Platoons were to seize the south bridge in conjunction with the armored infantry platoon, drive through the village, and capture the second bridge located about half a mile east of the village. The 2d Platoon was to follow across the south bridge, drive through the village, and block the road leading northward. The 1st Platoon was to follow and secure the south bridge. The tanks were not to open fire until they encountered enemy resistance.

Zobel did not send out any reconnaissance detachments because he did not want to attract the attention of the Russians. In drawing up his plan Zobel kept in mind that the success of the operation would depend on proper timing and on the skill and resourcefulness of his platoon commanders. Because of the swiftness with which the raid was to take place, he would have little opportunity to influence the course of events once the attack was under way.

At 0430, when the first tanks moved out of the woods, it was almost daylight and the visibility was approximately 1,000 yards. As the 1st and 2d Platoons were driving down the road toward Village Z, they were suddenly taken under flanking fire by Russian tanks and antitank guns. Three German tanks were immediately disabled, one of them catching fire. Zobel ordered the two platoons to withdraw.

Since the element of surprise no longer existed and the advance guard had lost three of its tanks, Zobel abandoned his plan of attack and decided to await the arrival of the main body of the task force. He reported the failure of the operation by radio, and at 0515 his units were joined by the main force. After Zobel had made a report in person, the task force commander decided to attack Village Z before the Russian garrison could receive reinforcements. This time the attack was to be launched from the south under the protection of artillery fire.

The plan called for Zobel's company to conduct a feint attack along the same route it had previously taken and to fire on targets of opportunity across the river. Meanwhile Company E and the armored infantry company were to drive southward, skirt the hill, and approach Village Z from the south. While the 3d and 4th Platoons of Company E, the armored infantry company, and

Company F were to concentrate their fire on the southern edge of the village, the 1st and 2d Platoons of Company E were to thrust across the south bridge, drive into the village, turn east at the market square, and capture the east bridge. As soon as the first two platoons had driven across the bridge, the other tanks of Company E were to close up and push on to the northern edge of the village. The armored infantry vehicles were to follow across the south bridge and support the 1st and 2d Platoons in their efforts to seize the east bridge. Company F was to annihilate any Russian forces that might continue to offer resistance at the southern edge of the village. The artillery battery was to go into position at the edge of the woods and support the tanks.

No more than two tank platoons could be employed for the initial thrust because the south bridge could support only one tank at a time. All the remaining fire power of the task force would be needed to lay down a curtain of fire along the entire southern edge of the village. This was the most effective means of neutralizing the enemy defense during the critical period when the two tank platoons were driving toward the bridge. To facilitate the approach of the tanks to the bridge, the artillery battery was to lay down a smoke screen south of the village along the river line. Having once entered the village, the two lead platoons were not to let themselves be diverted from their objective, the east bridge. The elimination of enemy resistance was to be left to the follow-up elements. The attack was to start at 0600.

The tanks of Company E refueled quickly in the woods, and the battery went into position. The task force was ready for action.

Company F jumped off at 0600. The task force commander and an artillery observer were with the company. The battery gave fire support against pinpoint targets. At 0610 the tanks of Company E emerged from the woods in columns of two, formed a wedge, turned southward, and made a wide circle around the hill. The vehicles of the armored infantry company followed at close distance. As the tanks and armored personnel carriers approached the hill from the south, they were suddenly taken under Russian machinegun and antitank rifle fire from the top of the hill. The commander of Company E slowed down and asked for instructions. The task force commander radioed instructions to engage only those Russians on the hill who obstructed the continuation of the attack. The tanks of Company E thereupon deployed and advanced on a broad front, thus offering protection to the personnel carriers which were vulnerable to antitank grenades. Soon afterward Company E reported that it had neutralized the Russian infantry on the hill and was ready to launch the assault. The task force commander thereupon gave the signal for firing the artillery concentration on the southern edge of the village. Three minutes later the 1st and 2d Platoons drove toward the bridge and crossed it in single file, while Company F's tanks approached the crossing site from the west.

As soon as the last tank of the 1st and 2d Platoons had crossed the bridge, the other two platoons of Company E and the armored personnel carriers closed up at top speed. The two lead platoons drove through the village and captured the east bridge without encountering any resistance. The 3d and 4th Platoons overran the Russian infantry troops trying to escape northward and knocked out two retreating Russian tanks at the northern edge of the village. Soon afterward all units reported that they had accomplished their missions.

The task force commander then organized the defense of Village Z, which he was to hold until the arrival of the main body of the 3d Panzer Division. Two tank platoons blocked the road leading northward, two protected the east bridge, two armored infantry platoons set up outposts in the forest east of River B, and the remaining units constituted a reserve force within the village. The artillery battery took up positions on the south bank of the river close to the south bridge. Its guns were zeroed in on the northern and eastern approach roads to the village.

In this action the task force commander made the mistake of ordering Zobel's advance guard to halt and refuel in the woods 2 miles west of Village Z. In issuing this order he applied the principle that tanks going into combat must carry sufficient fuel to assure their mobility throughout a day's fighting. Although this principle is valid in general, it should have been disregarded in this particular instance. Since the element of surprise was of decisive importance for the success of the operation, everything should have been subordinated to catching the Russians unprepared. If necessary, the advance guard should have refueled as far as back as Village X or shortly after crossing River A. Since the woods actually used for the refueling halt was only 2 miles from Village Z, the German commander should have foreseen that the noise of starting the tank engines would warn the Russian outposts who happened to be on the hill south of the village. A surprise attack must be planned so carefully that no such risk of premature discovery is taken.

Moreover, the task force commander should not have stayed behind in Village X, but should have led the advance guard in person. By staying up with the lead elements, he would have been able to exercise better control over both the advance guard and the main body of his force.

The attack by the fully assembled task force was properly planned and its execution met with the expected quick success.

TANK BATTLE NEAR THE
BERLIN HIGHWAY
(MARCH 1945)

By the beginning of 1945 Russian tactics governing major armored formations had improved considerably; however, even in the last few months of the war the general standard of training was only mediocre. This was hardly surprising considering the heavy losses suffered during the preceding years. Some individual units did, however, give superior performances. In this connection it may be well to remember that the sweeping successes achieved by the Russians during the later stages of the campaign gave their troops so much added impetus that the still-existing training deficiencies had little effect on the net result. An equally important factor was the steady decline of German combat efficiency.

In March 1945 the Russians concentrated strong forces on

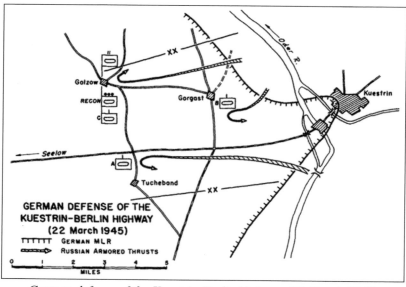

German defense of the Kuestrin-Berlin highway (22 March 1945)

both sides of the Oder River north and south of Kuestrin, which was still in German hands. From Kuestrin the main highway leads west to the Russian tanks were forced to withdraw. The second attack force, of almost equal strength, jumped off from the bridgehead west of Kuestrin and started to bypass Gorgast to the south. Just before the lead tanks reached the road connecting Gorgast with the Berlin highway, they were intercepted by Company B. The German tanks launched a flank attack which disorganized the Russian force and compelled it to pull back after heavy losses.

The northern prong of the Russian drive was meanwhile advancing straight across the fields toward Golzow, where the German battalion had its CP and which was held by Company C and the reconnaissance platoon. Although he had been informed of the Russian attack, the battalion commander stayed in Golzow instead of dispersing his forces in the immediate vicinity. This mistake was to lead to a critical situation.

Heavy Russian artillery fire prevented the German tanks from assembling in Golzow before pulling out. The general confusion among the Germans grew even worse when the Russian artillery laid a dense smoke screen across the eastern edge of the village. When the German battalion commander finally succeeded in assembling most of his tanks, he suddenly found himself face to face with a column of Russian tanks emerging from the smoke. In the ensuing battle the Germans were able to extricate themselves and stop the Russian advance, but solely because of the better maneuverability of their tanks and their superiority in close-range tank combat.

The Russians finally broke off the engagement and withdrew, leaving 60 tanks on the field of battle. Their failure to achieve a breakthrough in any of the three thrusts may be attributed to the infantry's inability to follow up and support the advance of the armor. In any event, the right-wing attack force should have bypassed Golzow and turned south in the direction of the Berlin highway instead of entering the smoke-filled town.

The German battalion commander had disposed his relatively weak armored forces as well as the situation and open terrain would permit. Anticipating correctly the direction eventually taken by the Russian left and center attack forces, he employed two companies to block their route of advance and deny them access to the Berlin highway. He kept the third company in reserve, ready to lend assistance to Companies A and B and to seal off an enemy penetration. His only mistake was in permitting his reserve force to stay in Golzow, instead of deploying it outside the village, as were the other two companies.

TANKS OF THE RED ARMY

Tactical and Technical Trends,
No. 5, August 13th, 1942

The New Heavy Tank.

Twelve months of war have brought substantial changes in the design of tanks of the Red Army. The new heavy tank has been named the Klementi Voroshilov, commonly referred to as the "KV", is 22 feet long, 10.9 feet wide, 8.9 feet high and weighs 51.2 tons. It has a road-clearance of 1 foot 4 inches, and can ford streams 5-5 1/2 feet deep. Its length permits it to span trenches 12-14 feet wide.

The "KV" is suspended on each side by six slotted wheels which give the outward appearance of double wheels. Each wheel is independently sprung on a rocker arm; the fin of the track is guided through the slot which prevents lateral distortion of the track. There are three return rollers and one idler wheel.

Improvements have been made in the track plate as well as in the method of interlinking them. There are no projections on the outside edges of the track plates on which snow or mud can become firmly lodged. The tread of the track has a grid pattern which insures a firm grip in snow and mud, and reduces sideslipping. Thus snow and mud cleats are not required.

A new method of joining the track plates has been devised. Each section or plate of the track has nine links which are interlocked by a full-floating pin. The pin itself is held in position by small disks or lock washers, these in turn held in place by a spring collar fitting in a recess between each of the nine links of the plate (see sketch overleaf). A broken track pin is thus prevented from working out of the links and causing the track to separate and immobilize the tank.

The contoured turret, cast in one piece, weighs approximately

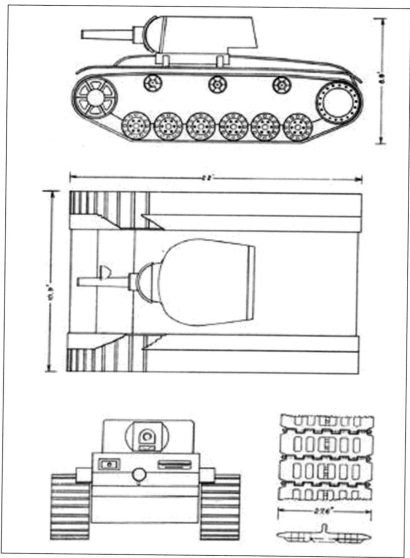

New Russian Heavy Tank (Klementi Voroshilov)

10 tons. The frontal armor of the turret is 3.54 inches thick, making it exceptionally rugged and capable of withstanding sustained enemy fire. It can be revolved 360 degrees either by power or by hand. Heavy steel bars laid on edge are welded at the base of the turret to deflect shells which might cause it to jam.

Following are the data on armament and armor of this tank:

(a) Turret armament:
- 76-mm. long-barrelled gun, (in some models of the KV a 152-mm. Gun is installed in a specially designed turret).
- One 7.62-mm. MG coaxially mounted with the gun

(b) Hull armament:
- One 7.62-mm. MG forward.
- Two spare 7.62-mm. guns as replacements for the turret or hull guns; or one may be mounted on top of turret for antiaircraft fire, or even used on a tripod for dismounted action.

(c) Armor:
- Front 90 mm. (3.543 inches)
- Sides 75mm (2.952 inches)
- Top 40mm (1.574 inches)
- Engine hatch 30mm (1.181 inches)
- Turret sides 75mm (2.952 inches)
- Rear end 40mm (1.574 inches)
- Under sheathing 30 to 40mm (1.181 to 1.574 inches)

Ninety rounds of AP and incendiary shells are carried for the cannon, the former being stacked behind the loader, the latter being distributed around the turret, under the floor boards, and in the driver's compartment. 3,000 rounds of machine gun ammunition in drums are carried in the turret.

The "KV" is propelled by a 600-horsepower 12-cylinder V-type diesel engine driving through a transmission and final drive to the sprockets at the rear of the tank. The motor is reported to be very noisy. The tank is equipped with both electric and compressed air starters.

It has five forward gears (four regular and one emergency), and one reverse gear. The tank carries 158.5 gallons of fuel inboard and can carry an additional supply in saddle tanks which can be discarded when empty, or prior to going into action. The normal range of action without saddle tanks is 110 to 125 miles across country. A maximum speed of about 21 miles per hour can be attained on an improved road.

The "KV" carries a crew of five consisting of the commander, driver, loader, gunner, and radioman. A mechanic sometimes makes a sixth member of the crew. The posts of the commander, loader, and gunner are in the turret. The driver and radioman ride side by side in a forward position.

The radio is in front on the left of the driver. The antenna is a vertical type mounted forward on the tank. Communication within the tank is by telephone. Inter-tank communication is visual, by either arm-signals or flags.

Tank warfare has taught the Russians lessons which have influenced their tank design. The turret is located well forward to permit tank infantrymen to use it as a shield while riding atop the tank. Every provision has been made to prevent unwelcome riders from getting aboard. There is a lack of external fittings, tools, sharp projections, etc.; this meets the double purpose of eliminating hand grips for enemy hitch-hikers and the chance that a fire bomb or other missile could lodge on the tank. The fender of the tank is very narrow so that "tank hunters" who seek to jump aboard run the risk of being caught in the track. The newer American sponson-type tanks have no fenders as such and have solved these problems largely through basic design. As a further protective measure for the tank crew, the hatch in the top of the turret is so constructed that it cannot be opened from the outside. A special tool is required to open the hatch from the inside.

The Medium Tank - T-34.

High maneuverability and relatively spacious interior arrangement have made this tank a favorite of Soviet tank crews. The Germans themselves have expressed the opinion that the T-34 was the most effective tank they have encountered.

The T-34 is a modified Christie-type tank. It has an overall length of 19 feet 1 inch and is 9 feet 8 inches in width. The low silhouette of the tank (8 feet 6 inches), beside maintaining 1 foot 3 inch road clearance, is an obvious advantage. The tank weighs

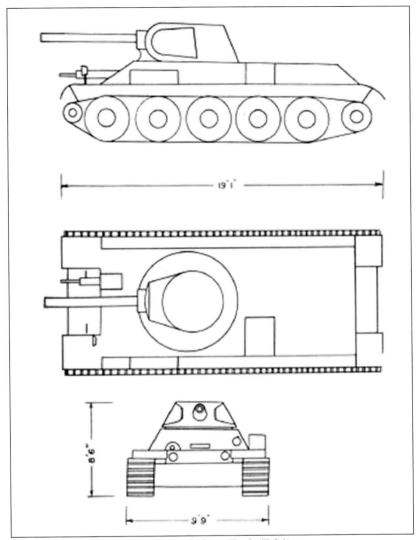

Russian Medium Tank (T-34)

29.7 tons and has a maximum speed of 28-34 miles per hour on roads and 18.5 miles per hour across country. It can surmount the same cross-country obstacles as the "KV" except that its length limits the width of the trenches it can jump to about 11 feet. (See sketch.)

The turret is of the built-up, welded type, equipped with two rotating periscopes mounted on top. Two visors, fitted with bulletproof glass are located on the sides of the turret. The turret may be revolved 360° to permit all-around fire.

The T-34 is powered with a 500-HP diesel motor similar in design to that in the "KV" and can be started either by electricity or compressed air. The track also is similar to that used on the "KV." It is narrower (21 1/2 inches wide) but has the same design and method of interlinking the plates.

Carrying its normal capacity of 120 gallons of diesel oil, the radius of operation of the T-34 is 150-175 miles. However, this range may be extended by carrying extra fuel tanks strapped to the hull above the fenders.

The tank is manned by a crew of four. The commander, who also acts as loader, and the gunner take stations in the turret. The driver and radio operator are in the forward seats of the hull.

Radio is used only to communicate with higher echelons. Inter-tank communication is by visual signal, while telephone and laryngophones are used between members of the crew.

Following are data on the armament and armor of this tank:

(a) Turret armament:
- One 76-mm. gun (for which 77 rounds of AP and HE shells are carried).
- One 7.62-mm. MG mounted coaxially on the right of the gun.

(b) Hull armament:
- One 7.62-mm. MG in front on the right of the driver (ball mounted).
- One spare 7.62-mm. MG.
- 3,780 rounds of ammunition for the machine guns are carried.

(c) Armor:
- Front 50 mm. (2.00 inches)
- Sides 20 mm (.77 inches)
- Top 20 mm (.77 inches)
- Engine hood 20 mm (.77 inches)
- Turret sides 52 mm (2.04 inches)
- Rear end 45 mm (1.77 inches)

The Light Tank - T-60.

The Soviet Light Tank (T-60) is essentially a gun carrier. It weighs 5.9 tons, carries a crew of two, and is powered with a heavy six-cylinder gasoline engine. It has a radius of action of from 75 to 100 miles and a maximum speed of 24 miles per hour. Its armament includes one 20-mm. automatic cannon and two 7.62-mm. air-cooled machine guns. The armor ranges from .6 to .8 inches in thickness.

The Russian Light Tank - T-26B used as a Flame Thrower.

Many experiments have been conducted by the Red Army to determine the advisability of converting the T-26B (8.4-ton) tank into a flame thrower. This tank normally carries two 7.62-mm. machine guns, or one 37-mm. anti-tank gun and one 7.62-mm. MG. If the tank is converted to a flame thrower only one machine gun can be carried.

On the experimental model of the T-26B, the (106-gal.) fuel tank for the flame-throwing apparatus was mounted on the tank instead of being towed on a trailer.

Various tests on flame throwers using crude oil (or some similar fuel) show that 10 gallons of fuel per second are consumed under high pressure through a 1.25-inch nozzle, to obtain a range of 100 yards. At this rate, the blast could be expected to last about 10 to 11 seconds. By lessening the pressure, the range is reduced to 25-40 yards and the stream of flame lasts longer.

The question arises whether it is worth-while sacrificing the fire-power of one machine gun for such a short-lived flame.

RUSSIAN TANK TACTICS AGAINST GERMAN TANKS

Tactical and Technical Trends, No 16, January 14th 1943

The following report is a literal translation of a portion of a Russian publication concerning the most effective methods of fire against German tanks.

For the successful conduct of fire against enemy tanks, we should proceed as follows:

a. Manner of Conducting Fire for the Destruction of Enemy Tanks

(1) While conducting fire against enemy tanks, and while maneuvering on the battlefield, our tanks should seek cover in partially defiladed positions.

(2) In order to decrease the angle of impact of enemy shells, thereby decreasing their power of penetration, we should try to place our tanks at an angle to the enemy.

(3) In conducting fire against German tanks, we should carefully observe the results of hits, and continue to fire until we see definite signs of a hit (burning tanks, crew leaving the tank, shattering of the tank or the turret). Watch constantly enemy tanks which do not show these signs, even though they show no signs of life. While firing at the active tanks of the enemy, one should be in full readiness to renew the battle against those apparently knocked out.

b. Basic Types of German Tanks and their Most Vulnerable Parts

The types of tanks most extensively used in the German Army are the following: the 11-ton Czech tank, the Mark III, and the Mark IV. The German self-propelled assault gun (Sturmgeschütz) has also been extensively used.

In addition to the above-mentioned types of tanks, the German Army uses tanks of all the occupied countries; in their general tactical and technical characteristics, their armament and armor, these tanks are inferior.

(1) Against the 11-ton Czech tank, fire as follows:

(a) From the front—against the turret and gun-shield, and below the turret gear case;

(b) From the side—at the third and fourth bogies, against the driving sprocket, and at the gear case under the turret;

(c) From behind—against the circular opening and against the exhaust vent.

Remarks: In frontal fire, with armor-piercing shells, the armor of the turret may be destroyed more quickly than the front part of the hull. In firing at the side and rear, the plates of the hull are penetrated more readily than the plates of the turret.

(2) Against Mark III tanks, fire as follows:

(a) From the front—at the gun mantlet and at the driver's port, and the machine-gun mounting;

(b) From the side—against the armor protecting the engine, and against the turret ports;

(c) From behind—directly beneath the turret, and at the exhaust vent.

Remarks: In firing from the front against the Mark III tank, the turret is more vulnerable than the front of the hull and the turret gear box. In firing from behind, the turret is also more vulnerable than the rear of the hull.

(3) Against the self-propelled assault gun, fire as follows:

(a) From the front—against the front of the hull, the drivers port, and below the tube of the gun;

(b) From the side—against the armor protecting the engine, and the turret.

(c) From behind—against the exhaust vent and directly beneath the turret.

(4) Against the Mark IV, fire as follows:

(a) From the front—against the turret, under the tube of the gun, against the driver's port, and the machine-gun mounting;

(b) From the side—at the center of the hull at the engine compartment, and against the turret port.

(c) From behind—against the turret, and against the exhaust vent.

Remarks: It should be noted that in firing against the front of this tank, the armor of the turret is more vulnerable than the front plate of the turret gear box, and of the hull. In firing at the sides of the tank, the armor plate of the engine compartment and of the turret, is more vulnerable than the armor of the turret gear box.

RUSSIAN TANK CAMOUFLAGE IN WINTER

Tactical and Technical Trends, No 17, January 29th 1943

The following report is a translation of a Russian article on tank camouflage in winter. The original article was written by a colonel in the Russian Army.

a. General

Winter camouflage of tanks presents a problem with certain special features, created on the one hand by the general winter background, and on the other by weather conditions which greatly affect the tanks themselves and their employment under combat conditions. In winter the change in the operational characteristics of the tanks and in the conditions of employing them in combat will influence the work to be done toward camouflaging them.

Winter conditions (as has been shown by combat experience) create considerable difficulties for the camouflage of tank units. In winter the principal characteristics of a region are its uniform white background, a lack of outline, and an almost complete absence of color. The only exceptions are small settlements, woods, and thick underbrush. Forests whose dense foliage provides perfect concealment in the summertime lose their masking qualities completely in the winter. In winter, on an even, white blanket of snow, camouflage is very difficult. Almost all methods of camouflage employed in summer prove inapplicable. It is necessary to make wide use of special winter covering for the vehicles, and to paint them with winter paint: all one color (protective coat) or in large spots (disruptive).

In winter, tracks made by moving vehicles can be easily recognized, not only from the air but also from high ground observation posts. The removal of tracks left by tanks is the personal responsibility of the commander of the tank units and of the crews. The presence of a blanket of snow, which is often very thick, greatly reduces the mobility of tanks, and as a result reduces the possibility of tanks appearing quickly and suddenly from directions unexpected by the enemy. Tanks cannot go through more than 3 inches of snow without appreciable loss of speed. The deepest snow through which a tank can go is 3 feet; for practical purposes tanks can operate in 1 1/2 feet of snow. It is apparent that these conditions greatly reduce the possibility of using approach routes concealed from enemy observation. Snow makes it necessary for tanks to employ existing roads, which means that they must engage in all their combat operations in those parts of the terrain which are under the special observation of the enemy.

An important winter factor from the point of view of concealment is the longer period of darkness, which helps to conceal the movement and disposition of tanks, provided, of course, that all camouflage measures are carefully observed.

Another winter factor which may be considered important from the point of view of camouflage and concealment is the greater cloudiness of the sky, which hinders reconnaissance activity by enemy aviation and sometimes stops it completely. Then too, tanks may make use of snowstorms which produce conditions of bad visibility and audibility, and as a result tend to lessen vigilance on the part of enemy observation posts.

b. Tank Painting

In winter, tanks are painted all white when the aim is to avoid observation, and in two colors with large spots when the aim is to avoid identification. As a rule, all-white paint is employed in level, open country characterized by a lack of variegated color. Two-color disruptive winter paint is used where the ground presents a variety of color, where there are forests, underbrush, small settlements, thawed patches of earth, etc.

One-color camouflage paint is applied to all parts of the tank in one or two coats. For the paint, zinc white or tytanium white is used only with an oil base, and slight amounts of ultramarine coloring. For the lack of anything better, the tanks may be painted with chalk dissolved in water.

Painting in two colors with large spots can be undertaken in two ways: one is to paint only part of the tank surface, leaving about 1/4 or 1/3 of the tank's surface in the original green; another is to repaint the tank entirely in two colors, either white and dark gray, or white and gray-brown.

When the weather is cold, painting should take place in a warm place, since paint applied when the temperature is 10° below zero Fahrenheit is too hard to be applied.

In winter, as in summer, it is necessary to avoid mechanical repetition of patterns and colors. For example, in painting the tanks of a platoon, one or two tanks are painted white, a third in white irregular stripes leaving parts of the protective green paint as it is, the fourth with white and dark gray spots, and finally, the fifth with white and grayish-brown spots.

c. Covers and Ground Masks

For winter tank camouflage, one may use nets made of cord which have fastened to them irregular white patches of fabric, about 1 yard across. A large all-white cover also may be used.

When using white winter covers, it is necessary to pay attention to the degree of whiteness of the materials used, for even if a little yellow shows or if part of the material is soiled, it will sharply outline the cover and the tank against the background of pure white snow. A simple method to improve this camouflage is to place a thin layer of snow on the cover.

In winter, ground masks are also used. But the construction of these camouflage masks involves special considerations dependent on the character of the background. The principal camouflage materials employed are irregularly shaped pieces of white fabric or painted white matting. In addition to the white patches, dark patches should be fastened to the material to give the appearance of bushes, tree tops, or other natural ground features. For dark patches one may use tree branches and other similar materials. As with covers, the use of white patches alone, or of a combination of white and dark patches, will depend entirely on the terrain and the coloration of the surroundings.

To attach the patches to the mask, they are frozen on after wetting the material with water.

d. Dummy Tanks

Drawing the attention of the enemy to dummy tanks has the same aim in wintertime as in summer, namely, to deceive the enemy concerning the disposition, types, and character of tank activity. However, in winter the making of dummy tanks is subject to certain special conditions. Large dummy snow tanks may be made by packing snow into the form of a tank, showing the hull, the suspension system, and the turret, and then spraying with paint. Movable life-size models are constructed not on wheels but on skis. "Flat" models may be made simply by treading the snow into the contours of a tank. In all other respects the making and use of dummy tanks in winter is no different than in summer.

e. Camouflage while in Motion

Generally speaking, winter conditions make it necessary to move along existing roads. Since winter roads appear to the aerial observer as dark strips, tanks which have an all-white winter paint stand out fairly clearly. In view of the fact that vehicles can be spotted by the shadow they cast, they should move on the side of the road nearest to the sun so that their shadow falls on the road, which is darker than the snow next to the road. Movement along the roads, especially at great speeds and over fluffy dry snow, gives itself away by clouds of snow dust. For this reason, movement of vehicles in wintertime should be at low speeds, especially over new-fallen snow. The tracks left by the tank treads stand out clearly as two dark parallel strips with tread impressions. These can be obliterated by sweeping the road. When tracks are left on the hard crust of the existing road it is necessary, instead of sweeping, to remove them with the aid of graders.

When the tanks pass through places where turns are unavoidable, there appear everywhere little heaps of upturned snow; these are characteristic marks and betray the movement of tanks. To prevent this, turns must be made gradually in a wide arc whenever practicable, or else the heaps of snow which are formed must be cleared away.

The reflection from the lenses of the tank headlights will also give away their movement. In order to prevent this, it is necessary to cover the headlights with white fabric covers, or some other material.

Finally, among the most important factors betraying the movement of tanks to ground observers is the clank of the tracks. [Russian tanks tracks are of all-metal construction.] The noise of these can be heard better as the temperature falls. Naturally, when operations are in the immediate vicinity of the enemy, one makes use not only of all the ordinary precautions employed in summer for the prevention of noise, but takes into account the special characteristics of winter weather with its increased transmission of sound.

f. Camouflage of Stationary Tanks

In winter, tanks are, generally speaking, parked alongside buildings and in woods and shrubbery; in exceptional cases it may be necessary to station tanks in open flat country or in gullies.

The peculiar characteristic of inhabited areas in wintertime from the point of view of camouflage is the motley appearance of the landscape due to the presence of dwelling places, barns, gardens, roads, and paths. This wealth and variety of outline affords considerable opportunities for concealing the position of tanks from air and ground observation by the enemy.

As a rule, all vehicles in bivouac should be placed under the roofs of sheds and barns. Only where there is an insufficient number of such structures, or where the size of the vehicles makes it impossible to place the vehicles in the existing shelters, is it necessary to build shelters, resembling the existing structures in the given locality. The roofs of these shelters must be covered with a layer of snow so that they will not look any different from the roofs of the existing structures. Just as in summertime, these camouflage structures may be built either as additions to existing structures or as separate structures. The separate camouflage structures should be situated along laid-out paths, and the tracks of the caterpillars which lead to the place where the tanks are stationed should be swept or dragged so as to resemble an ordinary road.

When there is not enough time to construct shelters, it is sometimes possible (as on the outskirts of a village) to camouflage tanks by simulating haystacks, piles of brushwood, stacks of building materials, etc. This is done by strewing over the vehicle a certain quantity of material at hand and covering it with a thin layer of snow.

Woods, orchards, and brushwood can be used for camouflage purposes in the wintertime only if additional camouflage precautions are taken. Since leafy woods offer much less concealment in winter than in summer and do not hide the vehicles from air observation, they must be covered with white covers, and there should be strewn over them broken branches or some other camouflage material such as hay, straw, etc.

When there are no white covers, the vehicles may be covered with dark ones, but snow must be placed on top and scattered. Dark covers can be used only against a background which has natural black spots. Finally, if no covers of any kind are available, the vehicles should be covered with branches, straw, hay, and the like, and snow placed on top in irregular patches.

When the tanks are stationed in open flat country, then the

camouflage of the tanks also involves the breaking up of the uniform aspect of the locality, which is done by treading around on the snow. Then these areas are given irregular form by scattering here and there patches of pine needles, straw, and rubbish. The ground should also be laid bare, as tanks which are painted a dark color will not be easily discovered against a dark background, either by visual air observation or by the study of aerial photographs.

In open country, thaws are particularly favorable to camouflage of tanks, for the disappearing snow exposes portions of the surface of the ground. The result is that the ground assumes a naturally mottled appearance, and the contours of vehicles stationed there are easily blended. When there is deep snow, tanks may be placed in snow niches built near snowdrifts along the road. The entrances to these should be directly off the road in order to avoid tell-tale tracks of the treads. On the top the niches are covered with white covers, or with some other available material over which snow is placed. In order to camouflage the entrance, it is necessary to use hangings of white cloth or painted mats which may be readily let down or pulled up.

When the tank is stationed in a gully, it is covered with solid white covers of any kind of fabric or matting painted white, or by the regulation net, with white and black patches attached to it.

RUSSIAN EMPLOYMENT OF TANKS

Tactical and Technical Trends,
No 18, February 11th, 1943

Soviet tactics, like German, are modern in character and show mastery of the entire gamut of weapons in modern war.

The following report deals with various items of information received from the Russian front, and is based mainly on articles which have appeared in the Russian Army newspaper "Red Star." No reference is made specifically to any particular phase of the Russian offensive.

The Russians declare that one of the main lessons of the campaign has been that armored forces alone can never achieve a decisive result; they must receive adequate support from other arms, and particularly from infantry, while they can never hope even to break the crust of a really strong position without the assistance of artillery or heavy bombing. The other arms are essential to deal with enemy artillery, antitank guns, and minefields. Moreover, even if tanks do penetrate a position, when unaccompanied by infantry they can be cut off and successfully dealt with, especially by night. The morale of seasoned troops remains entirely unaffected by the knowledge that isolated tanks are in their rear, for they realize that, provided the enemy infantry can be prevented from joining up with them, the tanks must either retire or be mopped up.

The Russians emphasize that armored vehicles must be concentrated to attack where they can be most effective. If they are supporting infantry they must be put under command of the unit supported, but the temptation to split them up into small groups with the object of helping the infantry forward all along the front must be avoided. Tanks should not be regarded solely as a means of direct attack to overcome strong resistance which is holding up the infantry, but should aim rather at breaking in where resistance is weaker, striking strongly defended localities only in the rear, and ultimately exploiting the "break-in" into a "break-through."

Tank forces in the attack must be accompanied by mobile field and antitank guns, which must be well forward to deal with surprise opposition. They will also be invaluable for repulsing enemy tank counterattack. Russian tank forces rely largely on air support, particularly by dive-bombers, to extend the range of artillery preparation, to harass enemy reserves, and to break up counterattacks.

TANKS IN NIGHT ACTION

Tactical and Technical Trends,
No. 15, December 31st, 1942.

The following report is from an article by two Russian officers in Red Star, an official Russian newspaper. It describes how a German regiment was dislodged from a strong position during night fighting.

***

Until very recently the extent of night tank action on the front has been limited to night marches, negotiation of water obstacles, and movement to jump-off positions for attack. On the field of battle, the tanks participated only from dawn to dusk. The opinion prevailed that at night the tanks were blind and would therefore lose direction, bog down in natural and artificial tank obstacles, and would not be able to conduct aimed fire. However, recent battles on one sector have shown that the effectiveness of night tank action is well worth the difficult preparations involved. The following is a report on one night action.

An enemy regiment had defended two important hills for some time. From these hills, he had good observation of our positions, which were on the far side of a river. Our positions were continually kept under effective fire. The attempts of the Soviet infantry to capture the hills were in vain.

The commander decided to attack at night. Under cover of darkness, a tank unit was ferried across the river, and concealed in a grove. The following day was spent in reconnaissance, and coordination and establishment of communications. The commander decided to send the tanks on a flanking movement from the south and the southwest, in order that the impression would be created in the enemy that they were surrounded by a large force.

The tanks were echeloned in depth. The heavy tanks were in the first echelon, the light tanks with "desyanti" (infantry mounted on tanks — see this publication, No. 3, p. 44) were in the second echelon, and in the third echelon were tanks hauling guns. The shells for the gun were carried on the tanks.

Three minutes before the attack, the artillery fired an intensive preparation on the front lines of the enemy, and then shifted to the rear, concentrating on the possible avenues of retreat. Zero hour was 30 minutes before dark. In these 30 minutes the tanks moved from the jump-off positions, reached the Soviet infantry positions, and moved out.

A full moon aided observation. After crossing the line of their own infantry, our tanks opened fire. The flashes of the enemy guns, and flares discharged by Soviet infantry aided fire direction.

The enemy artillery conducted unaimed, disorderly fire, and often shelled their own infantry. Pressed from both the flanks and the front, the enemy started a disorderly retreat. In 4 hours of battle, our tanks and infantry took full possession of the enemy strongpoint. After that the tanks maneuvered along the south and southwestern slopes of the hills, enabling our infantry to consolidate their positions. When it became evident that the hills were securely occupied by our infantry, the tanks returned to a grove to refuel, take on more ammunition and be inspected.

The German dead, the equipment left on the field of battle, and the prisoners captured that night gave proof that the night attack was a complete surprise to the Germans. The impression of complete encirclement was created, and enemy officers and men scattered in all directions. The enemy attempted a few counterattacks, but they were all beaten back.

In the following days, a few more night attacks were made on this and other sectors of the front. They were all successful and resulted in very few losses in Soviet tanks.

From the experience of these battles, the following

conclusions can be drawn.

(a) The attacks must be made on moonlit nights, when the infantry can orient itself and give the tanks the signals necessary for them to maintain direction.

(b) The tanks must be used in echelons. This allows movement on a comparatively narrow front, and creates an exaggerated idea as to the number of tanks in battle.

(c) Having occupied a certain line, the tanks must continue their maneuver so as to enable the infantry to consolidate its positions.

(d) During the attack, the tanks must under no circumstances be separated from the infantry. The tanks need the help of the infantry at night more than in the daytime.

RUSSIAN ARTILLERY SUPPORT IN TANK ATTACKS

Tactical and Technical Trends, No 34, September 23rd, 1943

The following article on artillery and tank cooperation in the attack is reproduced from the Soviet newspaper "Red Star."

When the fringe of the enemy defense has been broken and the leading formations advance to exploit their success, forward artillery observation is essential. Without this observation, fire from batteries in concealed positions will not be sufficiently effective to give continuous support to the advancing troops. The correct position of the artillery observer has, therefore, for some time, been with the leading elements of the infantry.

The problem, however, is to ensure powerful artillery support to mobile forces effecting a deep penetration. Single guns and gun troops accompanying these forces cannot always succeed in neutralizing enemy strongpoints of resistance. Tanks are either forced to stop or detour, with the result that the tanks are subject to serious threats from their flanks. Artillery time-tables prepared in advance, based only on reconnaissance data, are not sufficiently reliable, in view of the impossibility of discounting all the eventualities in battle.

Practical combat experience has proved that forward artillery observation is possible also in the case of thrusts delivered by tanks. This means that an artillery officer must be with the tanks forming part of the first wave. From this position, he will be able to judge what is holding up the advance; to call for and correct fire, and thus, although expending less ammunition, but achieving greater effect, the problem of providing fire support for advancing tanks is solved. At the same time, the possibility of shelling empty ground or one's own tanks is greatly reduced.

The experience gained by formations recently employed in the offensive on the (Russian) southern front allows for deductions of practical value.

In one case, an artillery regiment was allotted the task of supporting a tank formation which was to effect a deep breakthrough. The commander of the artillery regiment appointed one of his best officers, for liaison duty with the tank formation during the advance. Two days prior to the attack, this Russian officer became friendly with the tank crew allotted to him, learned how to fire the tank gun and machine gun, studied the probable course of the battle, arranged with his regiment the radio code procedure to be adopted for correction and control of fire, and checked the long and short wave lengths. From the beginning of the operation, he assumed command of the tank assigned to him.

As long as the tanks successfully dealt with targets with their own weapons the officer continued in his role of tank commander, and succeeded in destroying an enemy tank gun. Suddenly, however, the tanks came up against heavy opposition. The commander of the tank formation gave the order to move to a ravine for cover and allow time for straggling tanks to come up. The moment for fire support to assist the tanks had arrived. The artillery observation officer then transmitted his orders by radio. He directed and corrected the fire, as a result of which a concentration of two batteries succeeded in destroying the enemy points of resistance and permitted the tanks to continue their advance. Supporting fire was not restricted to opposition which was obstructing the advance of the formation to which the officer was assigned, but succeeded in providing assistance to formations advancing on his left flank which permitted the latter to fulfill their task.

A number of valuable lessons can be learned from this experience; first, the fact that forward artillery observation in mobile formations is effective is confirmed. As a result of the radio link the commander of the artillery is at all times aware of the position of the tanks and can provide coordinated and directed fire, taking fullest advantage of the range and trajectory.

This link is especially important when, due to weather, or other conditions, aircraft is unable to cooperate with mobile groups. Nevertheless, the organization of this type of forward observation required certain specific preparation. It is essential to assign as observer an experienced officer who is capable of orienting himself in any type of country.

Second, it is necessary to assign two observers to avoid any interruption should the tank of one of the observers be knocked out in action; furthermore, two observers enjoy a better view of the entire field of battle.

The position of the observer in the tank is usually beside that of the tank commander. Through him the observer can decide on various independent tasks, supplement and check the results of his personal observation and can restore communication with his artillery in the event of a break-down of his own radio set. It is emphasized that an observer should not maintain a position too far forward, from where the movement of the main mass of tanks cannot be properly followed. Observation is, furthermore, restricted, owing to the necessity of keeping the tank tightly closed.

The artillery officer is to be warned not to take too active a part as tank commander, and thereby lose sight of his main task. In pursuing individual objectives he may easily reduce his artillery to inactivity and the tanks will fail to receive support when needed. The observer's movements should be based on a careful and skillful maneuver giving him the best possible view of the field of battle, and he must remember that several dozens of guns are more effective than any one tank.

The method for calling for fire and correction is normal; by using a map previously encoded, the observer constantly pinpoints his position. On discovering a definite target he transmits by radio the nearest reference point and the relation of the target to it, at the same time indicating the type of concentration required. In adjusting the fire the observer indicates the correction in meters. The time of opening fire must be so selected as not to interfere with the movement of one's own tanks, unless these are halted in front of the target. The same principle is applied to the observer when putting down a barrage in front of his tanks or in parrying an enemy counterattack.

LESSONS IN TANK TACTICS

Tactical and Technical Trends,
No. 41, December 30, 1943.

Two examples of the use of tanks in conjunction with infantry and artillery were analyzed in an article which was published recently in Red Star. In one example the reasons for heavy casualties are indicated while the other example illustrates how a mission may be accomplished with minimum losses. A translation of the Red Star article follows:

***

The speed of forward movement of tanks on the battlefield is one of the basic questions of tank tactics. It is the tendency of the commander who has tanks at his disposal to make use of their mobility to increase the general speed of the unit. This policy conforms completely with modern tactics and should be followed as often as possible. However it is necessary to take into consideration all the conditions under which the tanks will have to operate. A tank maneuver must be well-prepared and it must receive all-around support. A few examples from actual combat experience may help to make this point clear.

A detachment composed of tanks, artillery and motorized infantry was ordered to exploit the success of troops who had thrown the enemy back from his main defense line. Specifically, the detachment's mission was to attack and advance 12 to 15 miles to the enemy's rear and capture a village, thereby cutting the route of the enemy's retreat.

The detachment started on its mission at dawn. The tank regiment, in march column formation, was in front. The commander of the regiment was told that security and reconnaissance units would operate along his route. Information concerning the enemy was very meager. All that was known was

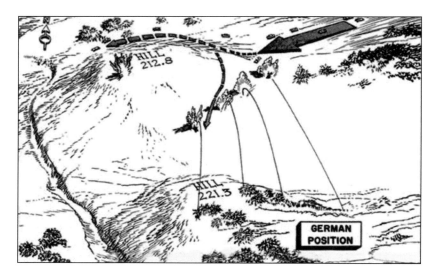

that our [the Russian] units, having driven the enemy back from a certain line of defense, were pursuing them in a south-westerly direction.

The tank regiment moved at high speed, preceded at a distance of approximately a mile by an advance group of four tanks. When these tanks reached Hill 212.8 they were fired on from the left flank and were forced to withdraw behind the hill.

The commander of the regiment believed that a reconnaissance detachment was operating somewhere in advance of the regiment, but he did not meet it. Later it became known that the reconnaissance and security parties had not been sent out; they had been forgotten in the general rush.

The commander of the regiment then decided to leave most of the tanks concealed north of Hill 212.8 and reconnoiter the enemy positions in combat. This was done with the help of one tank company (see illustration above). As soon as the attacking forces passed by the hill, they were met with flank and cross fire; also they were bombed heavily from the air. Some tanks reached Hill 221.3 but the company was soon compelled to withdraw. However reconnaissance data which was obtained made it possible not only to determine the general character of the enemy's defense but also the location of his artillery.

In the vicinity of Hill 221.3, in different places, there were 13 guns and 7 self-propelled mounts which kept Hill 212.8 and the whole field south of it under fire. In addition, five German tanks were located.

Without the support of artillery it would be difficult to break through such a barrier by a frontal tank attack. About half an hour would be needed to bring the artillery and infantry up to Hill 212.8 and to open fire against the enemy. Since the enemy defense to the right was not so strong, our tanks could pass around Hill 212.8 and by following the ravine could gain Hill 221.3 without much interference and then be in the rear of the enemy's artillery positions.

However, the commander of the main Russian detachment did not consider it necessary to spend time in coordinating his forces. Without waiting for the artillery and the mortars (only one battery arrived at the position in time) the commander ordered all the tanks to attack. The tanks moved forward, deployed in a line. As soon as they came up over the hill, the Germans opened intensive fire. To pass through the fire zone the Russian tanks moved forward at full speed and reached Hill 221.3 in a comparatively short time. The enemy wavered and then began to withdraw. A certain tactical advantage had been gained, but at the cost of unnecessary losses. Several of the Russian tanks had been disabled thereby restricting the possibilities of exploiting the advantage.

It may be said that this battle was characteristic in the sense of providing for a given high speed in the forward movement of tanks. The commander was right in trying to keep up the high speed of forward movement of the tanks, for the situation demanded it: but he made a mistake in hurriedly throwing his tanks against a strongly fortified antitank position. In such situations it is necessary to provide for the constant forward movement of tanks, not only to demand it.

The mistakes of the commander of the main detachment were as follows:

(1) He did not provide for proper reconnaissance during the offensive, with the result that the encounter with the enemy was unexpected.

(2) When the enemy's defense system and fire power had been determined, the commander hurried unnecessarily to attack with his tanks without the support of the artillery, of which there was sufficient quantity, but which had not been drawn up in time.

(3) The commander paid too much attention to the fast forward movement of the tanks and forgot about the organization of the battle.

Unfortunately, situations like this one above may still be found. There still are commanders who continue to urge on the tanks, at the same time forgetting the elementary principles of combat organization and the fact that time spent preparation will always be compensated tenfold.

In reviewing the battle we see that it would have taken only a half hour to organize the cooperation of tanks, infantry and artillery. This would have helped not only to deliver a telling blow on the enemy; it would also have provided the conditions for a quick and deep movement toward the objective. There was unnecessary haste in throwing the tanks into the zone of the heaviest antitank fire. This restricted their maneuvers and caused unnecessary losses.

In combat there are times, of course, when it is necessary to rush forward without taking into consideration many circumstances. However, in ninety cases out of a hundred, it is possible to find the time and means to provide for a high rate of forward movement without unnecessary loss. The best method for saving time is thorough preparation of the operation and its quick execution. This method is more to the point than an undiscriminating push which is sure to end in a sudden halt.

Some of the finest operations that have been carried out by our troops were characterized by thorough preparation and swift action.

On another occasion this regiment succeeded in carrying out an attack at a relatively high rate of speed. Here is a brief description of this situation and the terrain.

In the direction of the enemy ran a railroad track, along which, according to the initial plan, the Russian tanks were to attack and move forward to a certain village. There was a highway at the left of the railroad track. In front of the village there were several small wooded areas. Still nearer was an elongated hill which cut the highway and extended as far as the railroad track.

Having concealed his tanks behind the hill, the commander learned by observation that the Germans had several antitank guns along the road. Also signs of the enemy were noted on the outskirts of the wooded area in front of the village which was to be attacked.

The commander of the regiment was convinced that the movement of tanks along the railroad line would be difficult since the banks of the railway-cut were very steep and there were deep, narrow channels on either side of the track. He decided to send the tanks along the highway, where the terrain was most favorable. The infantry was to follow the railroad line, maintaining fire liaison with the tanks. The plan was to neutralize the German antitank guns, which were placed along the highway, by a sudden attack.

Results were soon realized. The tanks rushed at full speed into the antitank gun positions and smashed the guns, the crews of which had scattered. Without lessening speed, the tanks broke into the woods and exterminated a number of Germans there. Most of those Germans were having their dinner when the tanks appeared and so the enemy troops were unable to reach their guns in time to fight a defensive action.

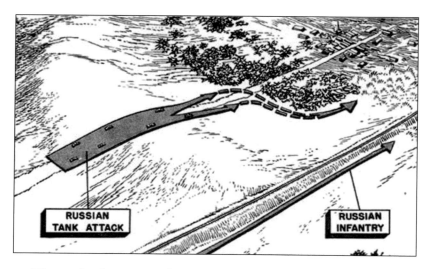

RUSSIAN
TANK ATTACK

RUSSIAN
INFANTRY

The tanks then passed around the right side of the woods and headed for the village but they were compelled to stop by swampy terrain (see sketch above). This gave the enemy an opportunity to bring artillery into action and open fire on the approaches to the village. Instead of forcing his way forward, the commander withdrew his tanks to a shelter behind the woods and remained there, awaiting the arrival of his infantry. Then both infantry and tanks, in close cooperation, attacked the village and drove the Germans out. Thus the objective was achieved.

In the first example presented in this article, the high rate of speed of the tanks did not reduce their losses, while in the second example the tanks not only succeeded in maintaining a high rate of speed but also they achieved success without loss. The reason for this was that in the first battle, suddenness of action was lacking, and also (because of the commander's haste) the tanks could not maneuver although the situation called for maneuvering. In the second battle the tank commander had ample time to prepare the attack well and to choose the most favorable direction. Although this took time, the results were excellent.

The commander estimated the situation correctly in general

although it might have been practicable to have sought a different route when the tanks reached the swamp. The element of surprise had run its course; further movement had to be based on close cooperation with the infantry. This was skillfully achieved, and at the same time the general tempo of the attack was not lost. After taking the village, the tank unit pushed right on.

In conclusion it may be said that at all times the commander estimated the situation correctly, acting neither too slowly or too hastily. Well-thought-out organization during every phase of the attack produces high speed in the forward movement of tanks, no matter under what conditions they may be operating.

RUSSIAN EMPLOYMENT OF ANTIAIRCRAFT GUNS AGAINST TANKS

Tactical and Technical Trends, No 7, September 10th 1942

Like the Germans, the Russians have found that it is profitable to allot antiaircraft guns a secondary mission of antitank defense. The following comments on antitank employment of these guns are taken from a recent issue of the semiofficial "Red Star".

"In the Russo-German War the Red Army antiaircraft artillery has learned to combat tanks as well as planes. Dual-purpose antiaircraft guns make good antitank guns because of their high muzzle velocity, high rate of fire, and 360° traverse.

"In the first 6 months of the war, Red Army antiaircraft artillery fired in self-defense at enemy tanks which broke through to the battery positions. Gradually, however, the antiaircraft artillery became an organic part of the antitank defensive system. In numerous instances, Russian antiaircraft guns have successfully repulsed attacks of large tank units.

"The antiaircraft units learned that most tactical operations seem to divide themselves into two phases. In the first phase, Russian army artillery concentrates heavy fire on enemy tanks before they can jump off. It then lays down a screen of fire to prevent the enemy tanks from approaching the Russian forward line of defense and breaking up infantry formations. In this stage the antiaircraft units are busily engaged in repelling the attacks of enemy aircraft, particularly dive bombers, which attempt to open the way for the tanks.

"In the second phase, after German tanks have broken into the initial line of defense, or deeper, the German aviation generally shifts its attention to Russian units reserved for counterattack. In this comparative lull, antiaircraft guns fire at the German tanks by direct laying; the shorter the range, the more effective the fire.

"It must always be remembered, however, that the first mission of antiaircraft artillery is defense against planes. In areas where there is insufficient antitank artillery, antiaircraft guns must be employed to drive off tanks which approach the battery positions or threaten to break up the battle formations of Russian troops.

"In order to combat enemy mechanized forces successfully, the antiaircraft artillery must prepare its antitank defense in advance. When the guns go into position they must be ready to open fire against attacking tanks immediately. To establish such a system it is necessary to:

1) Make a complete study of the surrounding terrain, with particular regard to possible tank approaches;

2) Determine the sector of fire for each gun, including ranges to key reference points;

3) Build the minimum amount of field fortifications necessary;

4) Establish special antitank observation points.

"All antiaircraft personnel not working at the guns during a tank attack take up positions in the vicinity and use hand grenades, gasoline bottles, or small-arms armor-piercing bullets against the enemy tanks."

TANK VERSUS AT GUN

Tactical and Technical Trends,
No. 41, December 30th, 1943.

In the following article, the Russian tank expert, Lt. Col. P. Kolomeitov discusses the current phase of the age-old contest between projectile and armor.

a. Tank Versus AT Gun

Which is the stronger — tank or antitank gun — armor or shell? Before the war there were different answers to this question. Some thought that in the contest between armor and shell, armor would be victorious; others doubted the possibility of providing a tank with invulnerable armor.

b. The Lightly Armored Tank

These conflicting opinions were reflected in the pre-war models of tanks. The basic quality of a fighting machine was considered to be high speed, on the theory that "the best armor is speed." And it is not surprising, therefore, that the peace-time tank forces of most countries consisted almost exclusively of light machines with armored plating from .236 inch to .630 inch thick. The war in Spain revealed the power of antitank artillery. The experience gained there was taken into account in all countries, but not fully appreciated by any of them.

After Spain there was a definite tendency to increase tank fire-power. As regards plating, however, no real advances were made. Preference was given, as before, to speed. During the invasion of France, for example, the Germans used the Pz Kw 2b, together with the Pz Kw 3, as their basic machine. The armor of the first type of tank was from .276 inch to .591 inch thick, and of the second, from .630 inch to 1.181 inch. [The maximum speed for each was reported to be between 37 to 43 mph.] To give some idea of their vulnerability, it may be pointed out that 1.181-inch armor is easily pierced by a shell fired from a 37- or 45-mm (1.457- or 1.772-in) gun at medium range. During the battles in France, however, the tanks were very effective by virtue of numbers and mobility. In other words, massed tanks were not opposed by massed antitank artillery.

c. Russian AT Gun Tactics

Apparently the Germans were thoroughly satisfied with the results of the fighting in France. They evaluated highly the battle qualities of their machines and considered them invulnerable. Disillusionment only came when the German tanks encountered Soviet artillery. The German tank divisions which advanced against the Red Army were chiefly equipped with PzKw 3's. With their aid, the Nazi generals counted on being able to swiftly and completely annihilate the Soviet troops. At the time it seemed doubtful that the swift iron flood unleashed by the Germans could be stopped.

The Germans were astonished at the power of Soviet artillery, and its ability to combat massed Panzer attacks. As early as August 1941 damaged Pz Kw 3 tanks were observed to have been hurriedly strengthened with additional sheets of armor plating which naturally reduced their speed. Nevertheless, armor-piercing shell could still penetrate the plating and wreck the tank's vitals.

d. Antitank Gun Wins

Victory was now with the antitank gun. No tank could face it without the risk of being set on fire at the first shot. New tactics had to be developed for the tanks; they operated in masses and carefully by-passed regions saturated with antitank artillery. Such tactics were, of course, expedient, but they definitely bespoke the weakness of tank armor. At the beginning of the war the basic antitank armaments consisted of 37- and 45-mm guns (1.457 and 1.772 inch) and also special antitank rifles, and tank specialists devoted all their attention to counteracting them.

Realizing that it was impossible to protect a tank against shells of all calibers, they considered it imperative to create a tank invulnerable to the basic antitank armaments.

e. The Heavy Tank

Such tanks later appeared — the Soviet heavy KV and medium T-34. In this way, Soviet engineers initiated a new trend in tank building. The basic types now became medium and heavy machines with thick armor, and yet quite mobile. It would be wrong, however, to imagine that tanks of the KV type are invulnerable to shells of all calibers. There is still not an invulnerable tank, and, perhaps there never will be. Yet the KV is but slightly vulnerable to the basic antitank armaments, and therein lies its strength. The best type of tank now is the one which combines the necessary mobility (about 24 miles an hour) with the strongest possible armor. If it is impossible to find an absolute protection against guns, then at least it is vitally necessary to reduce the effectiveness of the basic antitank weapons. One of the means is thicker armor.

f. German Innovations

Let us consider what the Germans have done to increase the protection of their tanks. A new machine, the Pz Kw 6 (Tiger), has now appeared on the battlefield. Its armor reaches a thickness of 4.33 inches, and it is armed with an antiaircraft gun of 88-mm caliber. This gun has been chosen not as protection against aircraft but on account of its range and the great initial velocity of its projectile.

The Germans consider that with the Tiger they had made a revolution in tank building. However, the Pz Kw 6 is in essence an imitation of the Soviet KV type. It can be safely said that it was really the success of the latter that induced the Germans to take up the construction of a heavy tank. However, there is one thing about the German Pz Kw 6 that merits attention. At first it seemed strange to arm a heavily armored tank with a long-range gun. Yet it was done in order to win superiority over enemy artillery and tanks.

The Germans thought that by opening fire from a distance of 2,000 to 2,500 meters, their Tiger tank would be safe from medium-caliber guns. Such has not been the case in practice. Of course, it would be a mistake to underestimate the power of the Tigers, but combat experience has shown modern antitank artillery is still more powerful.

g. The Contest Continues

The contest between armor and shell continues. In this, as in other spheres, tremendous progress has been made during the war, but the limit has not yet been reached. Simultaneously with the increase in armor there will apparently be a growth in the penetrative power of the shell.

It seems that the struggle between tank and gun will be ever-present. After all, every tank — for example the German Tiger — carries a gun that fires a shell capable of piercing its own armor.

SOME GERMAN BATTLE OBSERVATIONS ON THE RUSSIAN FRONT

Tactical and Technical Trends,
No. 23, April 22nd, 1943.

Below appears a translation of a German document discussing in outline form one of their later Russian offensives.

***

a. Preparation

Detailed preparation for the attacks was made possible through the constant collection of information dealing with previous actions, exchange of information between various headquarters and distribution of this information down to companies. Preparations included rehearsals over similar ground and under similar conditions; also, measures to deceive the enemy.

b. The Attack

The attack was carried out by surprise, with no artillery registration or preparation. The attack opened with coordinated fire on a narrow front from artillery and all smoke mortars and heavy weapons available. As success depends upon speedy removal of obstacles in depth, especially minefields, strong engineer elements were allotted to the leading elements. Cooperation with the air force was close. Flight schedules were arranged to leave sufficient time for refueling and resupply of ammunition. To avoid bombing of friendly troops, the air force was kept closely informed of the positions of troops on the ground by the aid of air-force liaison officers, and by ample supplies of cloth panels, etc.

c. Minefields

Minefields were quickly crossed by reconnaissance and by mine-detector sections, pushed well forward to mark the lanes.

Mine-clearing sections rapidly widened the lanes through the fields from 5 to 10 meters. Two lanes were made for each company sector.

d. Observations

(1) Whenever strong tank attacks were launched, the Russians coordinated the fire of all available antitank guns, and antiaircraft guns in an antitank capacity.

(2) The Russians would often let our attack come so close that our artillery could not continue to fire. Heavy weapons were therefore pushed well forward for use against positions where such tactics were expected.

(3) Mass formations had to be avoided in favor of organization in depth.

(4) When signal communications had not been set up, traffic difficulties were encountered between responsible headquarters.

(5) The use of the Fieseler Storch (a small liaison and command plane capable of landing and taking off in a very small space) was necessary for commands responsible for observing battle situation and directing traffic.

GERMAN CLOSE-IN TACTICS AGAINST ARMORED VEHICLES

Tactical and Technical Trends,
No. 23, April 22nd, 1943.

The following is a translation of a German document issued early in 1942. While some of the methods of attack discussed may have since been altered, it is thought that it reflects the essentials of current German doctrine. The preface explains the scope and purpose of the document.

Current Instructions For Close-in Tactics Against Armored Vehicles

Preface

These directives are based on experiences of the German Army in close-in combat against Russian tanks on the Eastern Front. The Russian tactics so far as known have been taken into consideration.

New doctrines of our own are in process of development and will be available to the troops after completion, together with directions as to their use. First, the Eastern Army will be equipped with incendiary bottles. Presumably the troops at the front use means of fighting about which, at the time of publication of these directives, no description is yet at hand. In addition, new enemy methods will appear, which will be adapted to our own fighting.

These directives, therefore, present only preliminary instructions. Cooperation of the troops in the field is needed for their completion. To this end, new fighting practices of our own and of the enemy should be reported, with drawings and descriptions of battle conditions at the time. Communications should be sent through the service channels to the General of

A German mock-up of T-34 tank, for training, upon a chassis of the Polish tankette TKS.

Infantry and to the General of Mobile Troops in the Army High Command.

The importance of close-in fighting against tanks makes it imperative that individual tank hunters be trained immediately in all the arms. The state of training in the Reserve Army will be tested by recruit inspections.

These directives apply to combat against all kinds of armored vehicles. For simplification, only tanks are mentioned in the text.

I. General

1. If there are no armor-piercing weapons at hand, or if their fire does not show sufficient result against attacking tank forces, specially trained, organized, and equipped tank hunters will have to assault and destroy tanks by close-in combat, making use of their special assault weapons and without waiting for specific orders. All other available arms will lend their support as strongly as possible.

Experience proves that with proper training and skilled use of close-in weapons, all classes of tanks can be destroyed by

129

individual soldiers.

2. Close-in combat against tanks demands courage, agility, and a capacity for quick decision, coupled with self-discipline and self-confidence. Without these qualities, the best combat weapons are of no use. Proper selection of personnel is therefore of decisive importance.

3. Thorough knowledge of enemy tank types and of their peculiarities and weaknesses in battle and movement, as well as complete familiarity with the power and use of our own weapons in every terrain, is necessary for successful combat. This will strengthen the self-confidence of the troops. It will also make up the crucial points in training.

4. Close-in combat against tanks may be necessary for all situations and all troops.

In the first place the combat engineers, and tank hunters are the mainstays of this type of fighting. It must be demanded that each member of these arms master the principles and weapons of close-in antitank combat, and that he use them even when he does not belong to an antitank squad.

5. Over and above this, soldiers of all the armed services should be selected and grouped into close-in tank-hunting squads consisting of one leader and at least three men. They must continually be ready for close-in combat with tanks.

Where special close-in weapons are not at hand, expedients should be devised.

Combining tank-hunting squads into tank-hunting groups may be useful under certain conditions.

6. The equipment for close-in tank hunting consists of the following: incendiary bottles and Tellermines, TNT, automatic weapons (our own or captured), submachine guns, Very pistols, hand grenades, smoke bottles, and camouflage material, as well as hatchets, crowbars, etc., to use as clubs for the bending of machine-gun barrels projecting from the tank. Of this equipment the useful and available weapons for blinding, stopping, and

An abandoned KV-2, June 1941

destroying the tank should always be carried along. In the interest of maximum mobility, the tank-hunting soldiers must be free of all unnecessary articles of equipment.

II. Combat Principles

7. Careful observations of the entire field of battle, early warning against tanks, as well as continuous supply and readiness of tank-hunting equipment of all kinds and in ample quantity, will insure against surprise by enemy tanks and will permit their swift engagement.

8. It should be standard procedure continually to observe the movements and the action of tank-hunting squads and to support them by the combined fire of all available weapons. In this connection, armor-piercing weapons must direct their fire on the tanks while the remaining weapons will fight primarily against infantry accompanying the tanks. It will be their mission to separate the infantry from the tanks.

Sometimes tanks carry infantrymen riding on them, who protect the tanks at forced or voluntary halts against the attack of tank hunters. These security troops must be destroyed by supporting infantry before the tank hunters attempt to assault the vehicles. Should the tanks arrive without infantry, the fire of all the available weapons will be concentrated against the vulnerable places of the tank. The shorter the range and the more massed and heavy the fire, the greater the physical and moral effect.

Fire by sharpshooters is always of special value.

The activity of tank-hunting squads should not be hampered by the supporting fire. The mission of such supporting fire is to split up tank forces, to blind and put the crews out of action, and to have a demoralizing effect on them, thereby creating favorable conditions for close-in assault.

In case fire support by other weapons is impossible, the attack by tank-hunting squads must proceed without it.

9. The basic principles of close-in assault are the same in all battle situations. In defense, knowledge of the terrain and of the time available will be profitable for the preparation and the attack.

10. The carrying out of close-in combat will largely depend on the immediate situation. The number, type, and tactics of the attacking tank force, the terrain, our own position, and the effect of our own defensive fire will always vary, and this variation will demand great adaptability and maneuverability on the part of our tank hunters.

11. Only one tank can be assaulted by a tank-hunting squad at one time. If several tanks attack together and if only one tank-hunting squad is available, then that tank is to be assaulted which at the moment appears as the most dangerous or whose engagement promises the quickest success. In general, the choice must be left to the tank-hunting squad.

If there is a sufficient number of squads available, it is advisable, particularly in defense, to hold one or more squads ready in the rear for the destruction of tanks which may break through.

12. Generally speaking, the procedure will always be: first,

to blind the tank, then to stop it, and finally to destroy the vehicle and the crew in close-in combat.

13. Whether the tank-hunting squads advance at the beginning of a tank attack or whether they leave their foxholes only during the engagement or whether the whole assault goes on from under cover depends entirely on the situation.

The behavior of the squads depends on whether the tank is moving or is voluntarily or involuntarily halted.

The attack on a heavy or super-heavy tank will often be easier than on a light tank, because the former in general is clumsier and has poorer observation. But the destruction of heavy tanks generally demands the use of more powerful weapons.

14. It is important in every case to make full use of the dead space around each tank.

In general, tanks should be attacked from the side or the rear. Any moment of weakness of the enemy tank should be utilized (i.e., impeded vision, halts, climbing and overcoming of obstacles, etc.).

15. Tanks should be approached by crawling and stalking, making full use of cover and concealment.

16. The foxholes of tank hunters must be narrow and have steep walls. They must be built without parapets and must not be recognizable by enemy tanks. They may be camouflaged either by canvas strips or branches. Whenever possible they should be protected by a belt of mines.

17. The tank hunters will remain motionless in their foxholes observing their targets and waiting in readiness for the favorable moment to assault. They must face the enemy tank calmly and must have the nerve to "let it come." It is always wrong to run away. While moving, the single soldier is inferior to the tank. In hiding, on the contrary, he is usually superior. He is safest inside the dead area around the enemy tank.

In villages, close-in assault of tanks is usually easier than in open terrain because of the abundant possibilities for hiding and

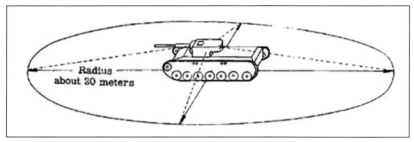

Figure 1

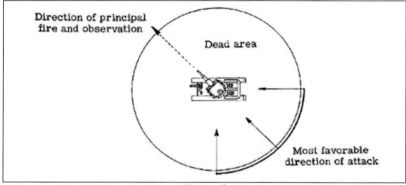

Figure 2

cover (as by roof-snipers).

Often the corner of a house, a bush, or a fence are sufficient as hiding places.

By the use of obstacles of all kinds, dummy mines and guns, and signs like "Warning — mines!", enemy tanks may be guided into terrain unfavorable to them, but favorable for the assault squads and antitank weapons.

18. When attacking moving tanks, the tank hunters at first must be well concealed and permit the tank to come close to them (7 to 20 meters); then they try to stop the tank by blinding it, or at least they force it to slow down. A strong blinding effect is obtained through the massed fire of all weapons. By using explosive charges, tank hunters destroy the tracks of the tank and cripple it. They will then assault it and destroy it and its crew with their close-in weapons.

In the case of halted tanks, the squad stalks up on it using the terrain to its best advantage.

19. Around every tank there is a dead area which it cannot cover with its principal weapons. The higher a tank, the larger, usually, is its dead space. In general, this space has a radius of about 20 meters (see figure 1). To combat targets in the dead space, tanks have slits through which pistols and submachine guns can be fired. Frequently a machine gun is found on the rear side of the turret.

When assaulting a tank, the tank hunters must make use of the dead space. They should approach the tank from the direction which is opposite to the direction of its principal weapons. This is also opposite to the direction of its principal observation (see figure 2). Should this approach be impracticable because of a machine gun in the back of the turret, the squad will attack from the side or diagonally from the rear.

20. The tank hunter with the principal close-in weapon will use it against the tank while the other tank hunters support him with their fire. Should he be impeded by that fire, it must cease. When the crew of the tank becomes aware of the assault, they will open the turret hatch so as to defend themselves with hand grenades. That instant will be used by the observing tank hunters to fire against the open turret and to wound the crew. Crews of stalled or burning tanks who do not give themselves up when getting out will be destroyed in close combat. If the tanks are still undamaged, they are made useless by removal of the breech-blocks, by destroying the machine guns, and by setting fire to the gasoline tanks.

21. Neighboring units support the attack by rifle and machine-gun fire against the vision slits of the attacking tanks as well as against accompanying infantry which might endanger the tank hunters. The tanks are blinded and prevented from taking accurate aim, and the enemy infantry is forced to take cover. Weak places of the tank are taken under fire with armor-piercing ammunition and antitank weapons. Lead-sprays entering through

the shutters into the inside of the tank will wound the crew. The cooperation of the tank-hunting squads with other troops in the area must be previously arranged, and all signals decided upon.

III. Close-in Combat Weapons and Their Use

22. There are several kinds of short-range media (blinding, burning, and explosive) which allow many variations of use. The type of armored vehicle, its position, and the terrain determine which of the available weapons are to be used, or if several should be combined. The leader of the tank-hunting squad will have to decide quickly which medium to adopt under the circumstances.

According to the doctrine "Blind, halt, destroy," the tank-hunting squad has to be equipped with blinding, explosive, and incendiary materials. Explosives have the double purpose of stopping and destroying the tanks.

Blinding Agents

Smoke Candles and Smoke Grenades

23. Smoke candles or several smoke hand grenades, thrown in front of the tank with allowance for wind direction, minimize its vision and force it to slow up.

Smoke

24. Common smoke is used like smoke from candles. To be able to obtain it at the right moment, distribute straw or other highly inflammable material in the probable avenue of approach, drench it with gasoline or kerosene, and ignite it with signal rockets at the approach of tanks.

The detonation of grenades and artillery shells also creates clouds of smoke. Moreover, the firing of armor-piercing grenades against the vision slits promises success.

25. When smoke is used, the tanks are hidden also to our antimechanized weapons, and they are unable to aim accurately. Therefore, smoke should be used only when the vehicles have come so near that they cannot be covered by fire any longer

without endangering our own troops, and therefore have to be destroyed at close range.

Signal Rockets

26. Signal rockets shot against vision slits have a blinding effect, particularly at dusk and in the dark; also, the vehicle is illuminated for our antitank weapons. Note that signal rockets only begin to burn at a distance of 25 meters.

Covering of Vision Slits

27. For this purpose one man jumps onto the tank, preferably from the rear, or approaches the tank closely from the side, and covers the vision slits or periscopes with a blanket, overcoat, shelter half, etc., or applies mud, paint, or grease. This is possible only if the tank is moving slowly or is halted, and if it is not protected by the fire from other tanks or following infantry. Any tank crew will be strongly demoralized by the presence of an enemy on top of their tank.

Incendiary Agents

Flame-throwers

28. Flame-throwers are aimed at vision slits, weapon openings, ventilators, and engine cover.

Incendiary Bottles

29. Incendiary bottles are a combat weapon used against tanks, armored scout cars, and other cars. In street and house fighting, they can also be used against living targets. They are thrown against the front part of the tank for blinding purposes, over the engine for incendiary purposes.

The contents of an incendiary bottle (not self-igniting) are 2/3 gasoline and 1/3 fuel oil. Ignition of the incendiary bottles takes place (when it has broken after hitting a hard surface) by the use of special safety matches.

The incendiary bottles are packed in wooden boxes in damp sawdust. The boxes also contain adhesive tape for fastening the matches to the bottles. The safety matches are packed in batches of twenty with 3 scratch pads in containers of noninflammable material. Two safety matches are taped to the bottle. The heads of the safety matches can be pointed either toward the neck or to the bottom of the bottle (see figure 3). The matches are lighted immediately before throwing the incendiary bottle, by friction with any rough surface or the match box. See that both matches are burning properly.

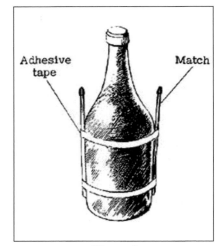

Figure 3

The bottles can be thrown in two different ways; throwing by swinging the arm, holding the bottle at the neck (see figure 4), or throwing by pitching, like putting a shot, grasping the bottle at its heaviest point (see figure 5).

Either of the two ways is practicable. In general, the position of the thrower will determine the type of throw. In a prone or similar position he will not be able to swing his arm, and therefore will have to pitch it. Whenever possible it should be thrown like a stick hand grenade, because the accuracy of aim is greater and the possible range will be increased.

The most vulnerable parts of a tank are: the engine (ventilation — on tanks usually in the rear), the vision slits, and imperfectly closed hatches.

Should an incendiary bottle miss and remain intact, it is better to leave it until the matches have burned out, as the heightened pressure might cause an explosion. The bottles should be handled with care. They should not be bumped together or against hard objects.

Improvised Incendiary Bottles

30. Any bottle can be filled with an inflammable liquid, preferably mixed with wool fiber, cotton, or torn rags. A good

138

Figure 4

Figure 5

mixture is two-thirds gasoline and one-third oil. Note that Flame-oil #19 is not freeze-proof. A mixture of gas and fuel oil can be used instead.

To ignite it, the bottle is equipped with an improvised lighter. It is constructed in the following way:

A wick is passed through a hole in the cork of the bottle, so

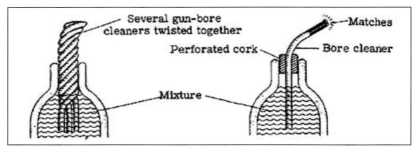

Figure 6

that one end hangs in the liquid. To the free end are attached several matches. Several wicks may also be used without the cork, if they completely close the opening of the bottle and are well drenched in the fluid (see figure 6).

At the approach of the tank, the wick is lighted and the bottle thrown. When it breaks, the fluid is ignited by the wick and is distributed over the tank and its engine. Generally the tank catches fire. If further bottles are thrown against the tank, they do not have to be ignited before throwing. Even initially a bottle without an ignition device can be used. After breaking the bottle on the tank, the liquid can be ignited with signal rockets, hand grenades, smoke candles, smoke grenades, burning torches, or burning gasoline-drenched rags.

Captured Enemy Incendiary Bottles

Bottles with a self-igniting phosphorus mixture (so-called Molotov cocktails) are used as explained in paragraphs 29 and 30. If large numbers of these weapons are captured, they should be collected and reported, to enable distribution among as many troops as possible.

Gasoline

32. Several quarts of gasoline are poured over the engine housing of the tank, and ignited as in paragraph 30. Gasoline can also be poured into a tank. It is then ignited by a hand grenade which is also pushed in.

Hand Grenades

33. Quite frequently an enemy is forced to open the hatch for

better observation. This opportunity can be used to throw grenades in a high arc into the interior of the tank. The crew can thus be eliminated and the tank set afire. Sometimes it may be possible to open the hatches with crow bars or bayonets and throw grenades into the interior.

Smoke Candle or Smoke Grenade

34. When thrown (as in paragraph 33) into the interior of the tank, they start the tank burning, or at least force the crew to get out because of the thick smoke.

Signal Rockets

35. Signal rockets shot into open hatches with a Very pistol can also start a tank burning.

Explosives

Hand Grenades

36. Several hand grenades can be combined into one concentrated charge (see paragraph 38).

One-Kilogram Blasting Slab

37. A slab of 1 kilogram [2.2 pounds] of explosive, placed on top of a tank, has about the same strength as a concentrated charge of 7 hand grenades and gives the crew a severe shock. Two such concentrated charges damage the turret hatch considerably and for a short time make the crew unable to fight because of the high concussion. Two or three such charges combined into a multiple charge can so severely damage the tracks of tanks that they will soon break under use. Even better are two such concentrated charges combined into an elongated

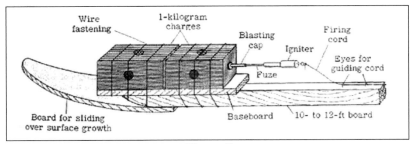

Figure 7

141

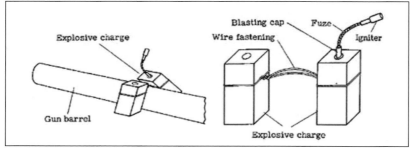

Figure 8

charge. For this purpose, two to three 1-kilogram charges are tied to a board with wire and equipped with a short piece of fuze (see figure 7 on previous page).

To destroy machine-gun and cannon barrels protruding from the tank, two 1-kilogram charges are tied together, hung like a saddle over the top of the barrel, and detonated (see figure 8). Machine-gun barrels are torn by the explosion, and cannon barrels bent sufficiently so that an attempt to fire the gun will completely destroy it. Inserting hand grenades into the muzzle of the guns also has good results against cannon and crew. Shells will also burst in the barrel if stones, wood, or earth are rammed into it. Placing hand grenades in the vision slits is also effective.

Several 1-kilogram charges can be tied together as a field expedient in case of lack of finished multiple charges.

Concentrated Charges

38. The bodies of seven stick grenades are tied together securely with wire so that they will not fall apart when used. Only the middle grenade is fitted with the usual handle with an internal igniter (see

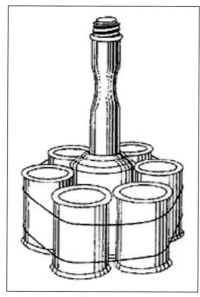

Figure 9

142

figure 9). This charge is ineffective against the armor or tracks of heavy tanks. But the concussion of the charge, exploded on top of the tank, will be so strong that the crew will be knocked out temporarily.

39. The concentrated charge of 3 kilograms, is found ready for use in the infantry engineer platoon, infantry engineer platoon motorized, engineer companies, and engineer battalions.

It will pierce about 60 mm of armor and is best placed over the engine or the driver's seat. The crew will be badly wounded by small fragments of the inner walls spattering off. The concussion is unbearable. To destroy the tracks, the charge must fully be covered by them.

Even greater effect will be obtained by combining several 3-kilogram charges.

40. The throwing radius for a concentrated charge is 10 to 15 yards. When throwing it, the soldier must consider the length of the fuze (about 1/2 inch burns in 1 second). The thrower aims at the tracks or at the belly of an approaching tank.

41. The concentrated charge can also be used as a multiple charge or as a slide-mine as described in paragraph 37 above.

42. If the charge is supposed to be used on top of the tank it must be secured so it will not fall off. For this purpose, its bottom is painted with warmed tar. If the charge is primed, be careful! A charge thus prepared will adhere to horizontal and even to slightly inclined surfaces. Putty can be used also for this purpose, but it is not reliable on wet surfaces.

Charges may be held on a tank by using an anchor made of strong wire, which is hooked into openings or protuberances of the vehicle (see figure 10).

43. The ignition for para-

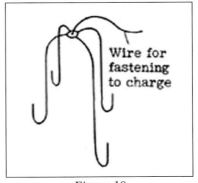

Figure 10

143

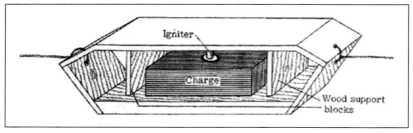

Figure 11

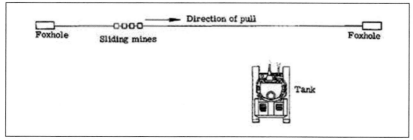

Figure 12

graphs 39 to 41 is provided by preparing short fuzes with detonating caps (to burn in 4 1/2 to 15 seconds), time fuzes, prima-cord, and wire for improvised pull igniter, or a pressure-igniter. The latter fastening is best suited for the destruction of tracks.

If the charge is thrown, a short fuze is needed (but at least 4 1/2 centimeters long, like a hand-grenade fuze). If it is placed on the tank, a 15-cm fuze is used for the security of the man placing it. [1 centimeter of fuze burns in about 4 seconds.]

Sliding Mines

44. Charges of 3 or 6 kilograms can be made and built into a two-sided skid. This sliding mine has to be secured against premature detonation, resulting from falling or turning over, by the insertion of two woodblocks (figure 11).

Two to four sliding mines are linked together and at each end of a given group is a 20-meter cable or rope.

Tank hunters sit in two foxholes about 20 meters apart. The sliding mines are camouflaged and placed somewhere between the holes so that they can be pulled in either direction. At the

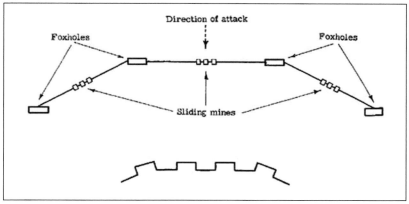

Figure 13

approach of a tank, they are pulled under its tracks (figure 12).

Several pairs of soldiers in similar foxholes can protect a larger area, for instance a key-point of resistance (figure 13).

Tellermines

45. Instead of concentrated charges, Tellermines [antitank mines] can be used, either as multiple charges or as sliding mines. However, as they have a high radius of fragmentation, they can only be worked from splinter-proof positions.

IV. Close-in Combat with Firearms

46. There should always be close cooperation between the tank-hunting squads and the other combat elements in the area. Discussion between the leader of the tank-destroyer squad and the leader of the other available arms is advisable in order to fix the beginning and end of the fire attack against a tank.

47. New [Russian?] tanks have especially strong armor at some points. But they have many weak spots, against which even the fire of weapons which are not armor-piercing can be successful. It is therefore imperative to hit the tank not only as a whole, but especially at those weak spots.

48. For this purpose, it is necessary that the rifleman, conscious of the power of his weapon and of his superiority over the tank, should keep cool. He must be able to open fire on the

tank as late as possible, surprising it at the shortest possible distance. Courageous riflemen with rifle or antitank rifle, making full and skillful use of terrain, should crawl up to the best range.

The shorter the range, the greater the accuracy of the weapon. Also, the armor-piercing capacity of the ammunition will be increased.

When using armor-piercing ammunition, in order to ensure its successful use, it is important to follow closely the instructions found in the ammunition boxes concerning the aiming points and the effective range.

Opening fire as late as possible has the further advantage of keeping the weapon concealed from covering tanks and observers up to the decisive moment.

49. Frequently it will be advisable to concentrate the fire of several similar or different weapons on one tank e.g., rifles, a light machine gun, a heavy machine gun, an antitank gun, and a light infantry cannon. Ambush-like concentration of all weapons to surprise the tank is preferable. The physical and moral effect will be heightened by such concentration. If only a few tanks appear, it is preferable to assault them successively according to the danger presented by individual tanks. In the case of a massed attack, rigid fire control must insure that the most dangerous tanks are attacked simultaneously.

50. When several different weapons are combined against it, the tank will be blinded by the use of heavy machine-gun fire and small explosive grenades. At the same time, guns of 75-mm caliber and larger will fire against the tracks to cripple the tank. It is necessary to wait for a favorable moment, when for instance difficult terrain slows up the tank, or when it halts to fire. Once it is stopped, it will be destroyed by combined fire or by close-in assault.

51. Weapons with armor-piercing ammunition of smaller calibers are sometimes ineffective against tanks with sloping armor plates, even if their power of penetration would be great

enough to pierce the plate if vertical. Because of the slope of the plates, the ammunition ricochets from the tank. On such tanks it is necessary to aim at the vertical parts.

Even in the case of vertical armor plates there will be an oblique angle of impact if a tank approaches at a sharp angle. In that case the angle of impact is also such that the projectiles will ricochet. Therefore, the tank should be fired upon at right angles. If the tank appears at an unfavorable angle, firing will be withheld until it assumes a more vulnerable position, either by revolving the turret or by actually turning and maneuvering.

52. It is possible to increase the effect and accuracy of fire by the selection of a flanking position, because the tanks are usually less strongly armed on the sides, and also offer a bigger target. Furthermore, vertical armor is more common on the sides than on the front.

53. Weak parts of tanks, against which fire from all arms is effective, are: vision slits, openings for hand weapons, periscopes, hatches, shutters, turret rings, ventilator openings, track, belly (the part of the hull between the tracks), and the engine cover (usually in the rear). The accurate location of these parts in the individual types can be found in the manuals.

54. Severe physical and moral effect can be achieved with the rifle, the light machine gun, and the heavy machine gun by firing heavy ball ammunition and armor-piercing ammunition at less than 300 yards against the weak parts of the tank, or by firing with submachine guns and armor-piercing grenades from a grenade discharger at very close range.

Projectiles hitting the vision slits or periscopes blind the crew, and prevent them from aiming or driving accurately. Also, small particles of molten lead and lead fumes penetrate into the interior of the tank and may injure the crew. Some bullets might jam the turret ring or weapon shutters so that revolving of the turret or firing the weapons will be made impossible.

As tanks are more poorly armored on top, attack from high

points such as trees or houses will get better results.

The demoralizing effect on the crew of the noise of bullets hitting the tank surface should not be underestimated.

55. HE and armor-piercing grenades (impact fuzes) fired with the rifle grenade-launcher (flat trajectory), antitank guns up to a caliber of 50-mm, the 75-mm infantry howitzer, and the 150-mm infantry howitzer directed against the weak parts of a tank will have about the same results as described in the preceding paragraph. Furthermore the power of impact will cause the inside surface of the armor plates to splinter off and wound the crew. If the projectiles have high explosive charges like the heavy infantry howitzer, the crew will become casualties from the concussion, or they will be at least temporarily knocked out.

When firing against the engine cover in the rear with explosive shells of all weapons, an incendiary effect may be obtained under favorable circumstances. Light and heavy infantry howitzers attack the tracks most effectively.

The ranges for individual weapons have to be selected so that great accuracy of aim can be achieved. For small dispersion and flat trajectory the light and heavy infantry howitzers should use the maximum charge.

The turret, the side, and the rear of the tank are considered weak parts for armor-piercing ammunition. Armor-piercing weapons, unable to use armor-piercing ammunition, can effectively assist in the assault against tanks with high-explosive ammunition.

57. Destructive results in combat against armor are obtained with the 37-mm stick grenade or bomb. Its short range, however, results in success only at close distances.

V. Training

58. Training in close-in attack on tanks includes the knowledge of the weak parts, of the construction, use, and effect of close-in weapons, and of combat principles. To this purpose,

instruction (using sand-table models and captured enemy tanks) and practical exercises are necessary. After the individual fighter has been trained, the cooperation of the squad and group in terrain exercises will be practiced. Combat exercises with live ammunition against large dummies or captured tanks will complete the training.

59. To improve accuracy in antitank fire, riflemen and gunners of all the arms (machine gun, antitank, infantry howitzer, field artillery) must know all vulnerable parts against which their weapons can be used effectively, and they must perform daily aiming exercises against tank models. Special practice is needed for the use of the Very pistol and rifle grenade. By the use of sub-caliber fire with antitank guns and practice firing with rifles and machine guns against tank models, and by combat exercises, marksmanship is to be developed to the utmost.

60. Each rifleman, whether he is part of a tank-hunting squad or the gunner of an individual weapon, must be thoroughly convinced that, if he fights skillfully he and his weapon are superior to any tank. He has to know that he is the hunter and the tank the game. This thought is to be given great weight in the training period.

VI. Assault Badge

61. The destruction of tanks in close-in combat counts as an assault. Riflemen, tank hunters, and other personnel who have fulfilled the necessary requirements in destroying tanks, will be awarded the assault badge.

ARTILLERY AND TANK COOPERATION - ENEMY METHODS

Tactical and Technical Trends, No. 32, August 26th, 1943.

In the following article reproduced from the Soviet Red Star, a Russian major emphasizes the decisive importance of close and rapid cooperation between artillery and tanks in the attack. The methods outlined are, in effect, an application of the same principle of cooperation so often stressed by the Germans.

***

Tanks are protected by armor, and are armed with guns and machine guns. In comparison with other services, tanks have many advantages in the way of maneuverability and striking power. Many military leaders placed all their hopes on armored forces, allowing only a secondary role to artillery. However, the experience gained in this war has shown that the role of artillery is not lessened by the presence of large numbers of tanks. On the contrary, it is increased. Tank attacks demand efficient cover by artillery fire. As a rule, tank attacks without the support of artillery come to a standstill.

Modern defense consists, above all, in antitank defense. The presence of various means of defense against armor, disposed along the front and in depth, well camouflaged, enables the defense to resist tank attacks in mass. To disclose and overcome all these means is not within the power of tank troops themselves.

Observation from tanks is difficult. Their range of fire is limited; accuracy of fire is comparatively poor. It is difficult to aim from a fast moving tank, which sinks into hollows and climbs obstacles. Forced halts even momentarily, increase the vulnerability of tanks. In such circumstances their advantages such as maneuverability, armament, striking power, cannot be fully utilized. Assistance is provided chiefly by the artillery.

The question arises of the efficient employment of artillery in support of the tanks. First, let us remember the varied nature of the tasks which the artillery can carry out. Artillery fire still possesses the greatest power and range. It can cover the movement of tanks to their assault positions, to their objectives and in the actual attack. It can put down concentrations after the attack, hold up enemy counter-attacks, and cover the evacuation of damaged tanks from the battlefield. The artillery prepares the breakthrough of massed formations of tanks, as well as assists in the movement of individual tanks. The methods employed are varied, depending on the size and characteristics of the task. Fire concentrations, changes in trajectory, lifting fires as the tanks move forward, displacing forward with the tank attack—all these may come into play.

The artillery missions must be planned for all aspects of the battle. The enemy will endeavor to forestall and break up our tank attack. For this purpose he will use long-range fire of two or three batteries, aimed at the route of approach of the tanks, at the areas of concentration and at assault positions. He will also use aircraft for this purpose. Therefore, the first task for our artillery is to cover the approach of our tanks and their concentration by means of counter-battery fires and antiaircraft defense.

While silencing the enemy batteries it must be remembered that long-range fire originates from reserve positions, of which there will be several. These must be located beforehand, so as to be able to reply immediately to the enemy's opening fire. Enemy batteries will not fire accurately without observation. Consequently, during the period of artillery reconnaissance of the hostile defense position and later, the enemy's observation posts must be destroyed or rendered useless.

Counter-battery fire must also be used after the tanks have started to advance. The Germans meet attacking tanks with a barrage at a distance of 2 1/2 to 3 miles. Our artillery must then endeavor to intensify its fire against enemy batteries, force their gun personnel to take cover in trenches, and hinder the enemy's fire control.

The principal and most difficult task of the artillery is to disorganize the enemy's antitank defenses. Often our gunners open fire against the front line of defense, thinking that antitank guns and obstacles are situated there. Actually, the greater part of antitank obstacles are below the ground, camouflaged. Ammunition should be saved at the beginning of the battle for a more opportune moment for destroying hidden objectives.

As the tanks approach the forward edge of the enemy's defenses, the work of the artillery becomes more complicated. The requirements are speed and flexibility of fire control. The tanks will be meeting with obstacles. Enemy guns, situated in the immediate vicinity of the forward edge of their defense positions will open up. Our batteries will have to change over to firing on the forward edge of the hostile position and their fire must accompany but not damage our tanks.

The method of accompanying fire is the systematic concentration on certain targets. The effort to attain accuracy must not entail any delay. Often a complete barrage of bursts is most desirable, especially as the Germans have now abandoned their system of an interrupted line of defense. Intensive fire, opened without delay, even if inaccurate, will reduce the effectiveness of his antitank defense.

When attacking tanks are accompanied by artillery fire, the latter is provided by all the guns giving close support to the infantry, as well as by part of the long-range batteries. The latter's task is, chiefly, to isolate the attack objective throughout the depth of the enemy position, to neutralize the reserves thrown into the gap and to prevent counter attacks. Fire is controlled from command posts, well forward. Attention must be paid to signals and fire correction by forward observers in tanks equipped with radio.

Targets which appear after a barrage has been fired, or targets which have been hiding in shelters, or defended positions which are situated outside the areas taken under fire, must be dealt with by support weapons. Such support guns accompanying the tanks must quickly destroy anything obstructing the tanks in their task.

After a thrust into their positions the Germans immediately organize a counter-attack with the help of reserves placed well to the rear. These counter-attacking groups consist chiefly of tanks. In one action, five of our tanks, accompanied by four guns, were counter-attacked by 18 enemy tanks. Our antitank weapons moved at a distance of 400 to 500 yards from our tanks. As the Germans devoted all their attention to our tanks, our guns opened fire on them. After firing 30 shells, two enemy tanks were on fire and four others damaged. The rest withdrew and our tanks successfully completed their task.

Recently, increasing attention has been paid to tank support artillery. Methods are being studied of the best cooperation with tanks. In this connection, the following is an example:

An infantry unit was ordered to capture an enemy position in a village. Tanks took part in the battle. A battery of 45-mm guns was detached to accompany the tanks. The guns were towed by the tanks by means of cables, and the crews, armed with automatic pistols, together with part of their ammunition were carried on the tanks. It looked like an artillery raid. Approaching the forward edge of the defense, and after taking the front line of trenches, the gunners shot up the Germans with their automatic rifles while defended positions were dealt with by the tank personnel. Later the tanks met with obstacles and the Germans started a counter-attack. Our gunners then unhitched their guns and firing over open sights, they drove back the enemy. This may not be a typical example, as these gunners were acting as infantry, but the fact that the guns were towed by tanks, and crews carried on the latter, is worthy of attention.

The usual method of moving guns behind tanks is for them to advance by their own traction, at distances of 200 to 300 yards from the tanks, in bounds from one position to the next. In this way the guns can cover the flanks of the tank units from counter-attacks and from flanking defense positions, which are the most dangerous of all for tanks.

SOVIET TANKS IN CITY FIGHTING

Intelligence Bulletin, May 1946

Special Assault Units Used in Battle for Berlin

In the battle for Berlin, a large city converted by the Germans into a fortress for a last ditch stand, the Russians used massed mechanized units in street battles. However, Soviets do not recommend that tank units be sent into the city, where movement is usually restricted and channelized, barricades and obstacles easily prepared, and every building becomes a potential strongpoint and direct-fire gun emplacement, but the lessons learned during the battle of Berlin are worthy of attention.

Writing in "Red Star," an official Red Army publication, a Major N. Novskov details what was found in Berlin, the difficulties encountered, and some of the methods used to overcome the stubborn German defense.

For the battle of Berlin, the Russians organized combined assault detachments, consisting of one tank battalion, a rifle battalion, a company or platoon of engineers, a battalion of artillery (not less than 122-millimeter), and a platoon of flame throwers.

"Berlin shall remain German!"—that's what the sign on the wall claims, but the crew of this Red Army 122-mm self-propelled gun had something else to say about it. It was with artillery of this type that the Red Army fought into Berlin.

Fundamentally, the defense of Berlin was based on three defensive belts, with intermediate strongpoints: the outer ring of defense along the line of lakes and canals: the ring of defense in the outskirts and suburbs; and an inner ring in the city proper.

The Germans had expected the assault to be made from the East and had concentrated their defenses in that area. Soviet tank units, however, attacked from the south, cutting off the Berlin garrison from the southern German armies which were to have constituted its defense in that sector. The attack in the southern sector moved swiftly, with the Soviets by-passing the main centers of resistance and driving quickly through the outskirts and into the suburbs.

One big obstacle that had to be countered in this first phase was the crossing of the Teltow Canal, where the Germans had demolished all the bridges or had prepared them for demolition. After a thorough reconnaissance, a well organized and coordinated assault was made on the canal and a crossing effected.

In the suburbs, the tanks had a certain degree of maneuverability, due to the larger number of gardens, squares, parks, and athletic fields. They were able to by-pass and envelop separate centers of resistance, to attack some defense fortifications from the rear, and to complete enveloping movements in some cases. Once enveloped, the defense zones in this area quickly collapsed.

In the center of the city, the nature of the fighting was quite different from the fighting in the suburban area. Many-storied buildings in solid masses reduced the maneuverability of tank units. The only avenues of advance were along the streets from building to building. Maneuver was not entirely prohibited, however, for heavily barricaded streets and strongpoints could be enveloped by way of adjacent buildings.

During the battle for the center of the city, the tanks were used in a supporting role to reinforce the infantry and artillery. The

A group of Soviet 152-mm self-propelled gun-howitzers halt on the side of an avenue during the fight for Berlin. The Red Army broke into the German capital by using detachments of tanks, assault guns, infantry, and support troops.

infantry cleared the buildings of antitank gunners who were concealed in the basements or in the lower floors. After the buildings had been cleared, the tanks would advance.

It was in this battle for the center of the city that the combined assault detachments proved their worth. The combined detachment was able to attack with well protected flanks, and could maneuver within the limits of two or three buildings.

The general plan of operations of the assault detachments was as follows: If the detachment met with obstructions, it by-passed the obstruction, or the sappers would blow up the obstacle under the cover of tank and infantry fire. At the same time, the artillery placed fire on the buildings beyond the obstruction, thus blinding the enemy defense and providing additional cover under which the flame throwers set the buildings afire. After demolition of the obstruction, the tanks then rushed forward and tried to get past the enemy defense zone, while the infantry cleared the enemy from the zone itself. Flanks were protected along the side streets by self-propelled mounts or by tanks.

This basic plan was, of course, subject to variation. Depending upon a number of elements, such as the nature of the enemy fortifications, the enemy power of resistance, and the composition of the attacking elements, the tank battalion can attack along two or three streets. Major Novskov asserts that it is better to attack along three streets, keeping the reserve in the center. When the attack is successful along any of the streets, the attacking force is then able to maneuver and envelope the stronger portion of the defensive zone. A tank attack along a larger number of streets leads to a dispersal of force and a reduction in the rate of attack.

Each tank brigade ordinarily had as a main objective the envelopment of from four to six buildings. In the accomplishment of its mission it was found to be of special importance to have a mobile reserve capable of commitment in the direction of the main effort.

Red Army T-34 tanks rendezvous in the rubble of a Berlin square. During combat in the city, Soviet tank battalions, supported by infantry, assault guns, and engineers, attacked on an average front of two to three city streets wide.

Major Novskov states that the boldness of the tankmen played a great role in the street battles. When artificial obstructions were not present, the tanks, with motorized infantry dismounting at high speed, dashed through certain buildings to intersections, squares, or parks, where they took up positions and waited for the infantry. When the infantry had cleared the enemy from the buildings that had been passed by the tanks, the tanks again moved forward in the same manner. When a defended obstacle was encountered, the tank first tried to by-pass it. When it proved to be impossible to by-pass the obstacle, and only when it was impossible, they would begin assault operations.

An example of the action of one assault group is cited by Major Novskov. "While attacking in the direction of the Ringbahn (loop railroad), the tank battalion was stopped in the northern part of Mecklenburgische Strasse by a reinforced

159

concrete wall 8 meters wide and 2.5 meters high. The barricade was protected by strong machine gun and automatic fire and also by antitank grenade launchers installed in houses at the barricade itself. There were no detours. The commander decided to break through the obstacle. He first sent out a group of submachine gunners whose mission was to annihilate the grenade launchers, which was accomplished in a short period of time. Then 122-millimeter guns opened fire on the houses where the enemy firing points were located. The tanks, advancing simultaneously with the artillery, also opened fire on the buildings on the other side of the barricade. Under cover of the artillery and tank fire assault engineers climbed up to the barricade with explosives. After three explosions in the barricade, a breach was made through which tanks and infantry rushed. The well organized mutual support guaranteed the success of the attack."

In the case of Berlin, used as an example of a large modern city turned into a fortress, the Russians emphasize the importance of mobile reserves; the formation of cooperating teams of tanks, infantry, artillery, and engineers; the importance of heavy artillery ("not less than 122-millimeter"); and the fact that maneuver though restricted by the channelized avenues of advance, can still be performed on a limited scale.

The Soviets further note that the use of massed tanks in the streets of a modern city is not recommended, but that it has been done, and tanks can be used effectively if it is done correctly.

They emphasize the importance of not dispersing the attacking force too greatly, and of attacking on a relatively narrow front for each assault detachment.

GERMAN COMMENT ON ENEMY TANKS

Tactical and Technical Trends, No. 35, October 7th, 1943

A critical study of French, British, Russian and American tanks was published on 27 June 1943 in the German weekly newspaper Das Reich. It is interesting to note that the author does not attempt to minimize the merits of American tanks, particularly the General Sherman, and that he concedes that German soldiers "know the dangers represented by these tanks when they appear in large numbers." A translation of the Das Reich article follows:

***

The German High Command maintains a museum of captured tanks — or one might say a kind of technical school where some of our most highly skilled engineers and a number of officers specially chosen for the purpose are testing those monsters of the enemy's battle cavalry, testing their adaptability to the terrain, their power of resistance to attack, and their special qualities suiting them for employment in attack. These tests are carried out in a forest region of central Germany where the terrain up-hill and down-hill is intersected by ravines and all manner of depressions of the ground. The results are embodied in long tabulations not unlike those prepared by scientific laboratories, and in recommendation to the designers of German counter-weapons, who pass them on to the tank factories and armament shops. The type of combat actually carried on at the front is reenacted here in make-believe encounters worked out to the last point of refinement.

The officer in charge of these experiments has developed a thesis which is extremely interesting, even though higher headquarters are not, without exception, in agreement with him. He contends that the various types of tanks reflect psychological traits of the nations that produced them.

The French have produced a number of unmaneuverable but thickly armored "chars" embodying the French doctrine of defense. They are conceived as solid blocks of iron to assist the troops in rendering the solidified defensive front even more rigid. The Renault and Hotchkiss types of tanks have indirectly contributed toward stagnation of the military situation. It was out of the question for these French tanks to swarm forth in conquest into the plains of enemy territory, dashing madly ahead for distances of hundreds of kilometers. Their crews normally consisted of only two men each. It was impossible for these tanks to cooperate as members of a complex formation. Communication from one tank to another was limited to the primitive method of looking through peepholes in these cells of steel.

The French still have, from the period shortly after the first World War, a 72-ton dreadnaught, the weight of which is distributed over the length of three to four railroad undertrucks; it carries a crew of thirteen; but its armor is of a type that simply falls apart like so much tin under fire from a modern cannon. As late as 1940 there were those in France who demanded increasing numbers of these rolling dry-land ships and wanted them to be of stronger construction than ever before. But German troops encountered these 72-ton tanks only in the form of immobile freight shipments not yet unloaded in the combat zones.

In the opinion of experts, English tanks of the cruiser class come much nearer to satisfying requirements of a proper tank for practical use in the present war. The name in itself indicates that the basic idea was carried over from naval construction. These tanks are equipped with a good motor and are capable of navigating through large areas. The amount of armor was

A KV-1 on fire, knocked out near Voronezh in 1942.

reduced for the sake of higher speed and greater cruising radius. Tactically these tanks are more or less a counterpart of torpedo destroyer formations, out on the endless spaces of ocean. They are best adapted — and this is quite a significant factor — to the hot and sparsely settled areas of the English colonial empire. The English tank is an Africa tank. It has a narrow tread chain. It did not come much into the foreground on the European continent. A tank for use in Europe, apparently, is something for which the English don't show so much talent.

On Soviet territory the English tank was a failure; and it shares this fate with the North American tanks, which were not appreciated very much by the Soviet ally. These North American tanks include, for instance, the "General Stuart," a reconnaissance and rear-guard tank, bristling with machine-guns, as well as the "General Lee." Although the latter possesses commendable motor qualities, its contours are not well balanced, and its silhouette is bizarre and too tall.

This criticism does not apply, however, to the most recent North American development, the "General Sherman." The latter represents one of the special accomplishments of the North

American laboratories. With its turtle-shaped crown rising in one piece above the "tub" and turret it must be regarded as quite a praiseworthy product of the North American steel industry. The first things to attract attention are serial construction and fulfillment of the almost arrogant requirements of the North American automobile industry as regards speed, smooth riding, and streamlined contour of the ensemble. It is equipped with soft rubber boots, that is with rubber padding on the individual treads of the caterpillar mechanism. It seems largely intended for a civilized landscape or, to put the matter in terms of strategy, for thoroughly cultivated areas in Tunisian Africa and for the invasion of Europe. It represents the climax of the enemy's accomplishments in this line of production. But we cannot gain quite the proper perspective until we examine also the tank production of the Soviets.

The T-34 used by the Russians at the opening of hostilities in 1941 was at that time the best tank produced anywhere — with its 76-mm long-barrelled gun its tightfitting tortoise-shaped cap, the slanting sides of its "tub," the broad cat's-paw tread of its forged caterpillar chains capable of carrying this 26-ton tank across swamps and morasses no less than through the grinding sands of the steppes. In this matter the Soviet Union does not appear in the role of the exploited proletarian, but rather as an exploiter of all the varied branches of capitalistic industry and invention. Some of the apparatus was so closely copied after German inventions that the German Bosch Company was able to build its own spare parts unmodified into the Soviet-constructed apparatus.

The Soviet Union was the only nation in the world to possess, even prior to the approach of the present war, completely perfected and tried-out series of tanks. The Soviets had such tanks, for instance, in the autumn of 1932. Basing their procedure on experience gained in maneuvers, the Russians then developed independently additional new series, building to some extent on advances abroad, like those embodied in the fast Christie tank (speed 90 to 110 km.) of the North Americans.

Like Germany and England, the Soviet Union thereupon hit upon a tank constructed for employment in separate operational units. Groups of these tanks operate in isolation in advanced zones of combat, at increasing distances from the infantry. Only a minor tank force is thrown into action for tactical cooperation with infantry forces. Such, at least, was the idea. And in fact, the T-34 was found suited for this type of action — though in many instances only by way of covering a retreat. But even for this type of tank, positional warfare has in many instances had the result of narrowing the designer's and the strategist's operational conception to the narrower range of tactical employment.

The Soviet Union also has constructed an imitation — in fact two imitations — of an amphibian tank built by Vickers-Armstrong. Another variant of Soviet thought on the subject came to the fore when the Russians constructed a 52-ton land battleship with 3 turrets, a vehicle of quite impressive appearance but provided with walls that were not stout enough to serve the purpose. The first of these monsters broke down in the mud a short distance behind Lemberg, in 1941. After that they were found more and more rarely; and at last they dropped out altogether.

In order properly to evaluate the most recent tank creations, such as the North American "General Sherman" or the German "Tiger", one must learn to view a tank as embodying a combination of firing power, speed, and resistance or, to express the same idea more concretely, as a combination of cannon, motor, and armor. In this type of construction, the paradoxes involved in the ordinary problems of automobile body building are raised to their highest potential. A mere addition to one of the above-indicated dimensions, let us say the motor by itself or the armor by itself, is not apt to be of value.

A fast-moving tank must not weigh much, and heavy armor

does not ride well. The caliber of the cannon affects the size and weight of its ammunition; and a difference in the latter is usually multiplied about a hundredfold, since tanks usually carry about 100 rounds as reserve ammunition. Taking all these things into consideration, we look upon the "General Sherman" as embodying a type of strategy that is conceived in terms of movement: it is a "running" tank, all the more since the Americans most likely expected to use it on readily passable terrain, that is on European soil. The caliber of its principal weapon is slightly in excess of the maximum so far attained by the foreign countries. It is spacious inside. Its aeroplane motor is of light weight. It is a series product, the same as its cast-steel coat, the latter being modeled into an almost artistic-looking contour, in such manner as to offer invariably a curved, that is a deflecting surface to an approaching bullet.

In Tunis, German soldiers have demonstrated their ability to deal with this tank; but they know the danger represented by these tanks when they appear in large herds. An imposing innovation is the stabilization equipment of the cannon. This equipment is connected with a system of gyros and permits even and smooth laying of the gun. This system was taken over from naval artillery and applied to the shocks incident to swaying over uneven terrain, where stabilization, of course, represents a far more difficult problem. This is the first attempt of its kind ever to be made anywhere.

RUSSIAN ANTITANK TACTICS

1. INTRODUCTION

The Russian Army had forced upon it in June 1941 the major portion of Germany's armored forces. The Russians were driven back several hundred miles eastward during the first few months of the campaign, but, at the same time, they were studying the German tactics. And in the fall of 1941, when the Germans made an all-out attack for Moscow, the Soviets put into effect certain antitank tactics that finally halted the German drive.

These tactics, in general, involve placing the various antitank weapons in considerable depth and supporting them with heavy artillery, infantry, and frequently with aircraft. They are designed to break up the massed attacks made at relatively weak points by German tanks.

2. VARIOUS METHODS EMPLOYED

a. Organization of Terrain

Selection of terrain which limits or prevents the maneuvering of tanks is a major factor in breaking up armored attacks. In fact, the Russians consider that denial of maneuverability is half the battle—the enemy must not be allowed to choose his ground or the time of attack.

The Russian defenses against armored vehicles are based mainly on "islands of resistance" disposed in depth. More often than not, these areas of resistance are centered around towns and villages or other built-up places. The Russians acquired considerable experience in organizing defenses in towns and villages during the revolutionary and Polish campaigns of 1918-1921. Their facilities for such defensive activity have been increased since that time by the systematic training of women and children, who operate the aircraft warning system, help to organize the defenses, and sometimes act as snipers.

To consolidate a town's defenses, armed detachments of soldiers and civilians are disposed at strategically important sites. Stone dwellings are used for emplacing heavy machine guns, either on the roofs or through windows. Antitank and antiaircraft guns are emplaced so that they can be fired down roads or streets, along with machine-gun fire. Tank mines and barriers are placed along likely approaches. Barricades are constructed for street fighting in case a penetration should occur.

Over areas selected for defense against tanks, the Russians frequently construct thousands of X-shaped tank obstacles by crossing three pieces of heavy steel rails or beams, and by driving them partly into the ground or wiring them together on top of the ground. Tanks approaching these obstacles must either slow down or maneuver around them. Artillery is sited to open fire as the tanks approach the obstacles — which, therefore, serve much the same purpose as the British minefields in North Africa.

Well in advance of their defended positions, the Russians install thousands of prefabricated individual concrete pillboxes. These are moved on trucks to the areas which need them. Holes are dug into the ground according to a planned scheme, and the pillboxes are then dropped into the holes. The pillboxes are distributed in great depth along the main highways. They are arranged so that an enemy, concentrating on destroying a certain pillbox, encounters oblique or flanking fire from others.

b. Use of Artillery

The Russians rely on artillery as their main weapon in fighting tanks. They make particular use of an 85-mm dual-purpose gun. Other pieces used extensively include 76-mm and 45-mm guns.

Usually the artillery opens up with long-range fire against moving or assembling tanks. Barrages are employed to disorganize tank combat formations, to cause casualties, and to separate the tanks from the infantry and accompanying artillery. In addition to stationary guns, a mobile reserve of antitank guns is always available.

If the Germans are able to attack after the long-range shelling, the Russians do not put their antitank system into effect until the tanks cross their line of departure and break through the forward positions.

How the Russians emplace their 45-mm and 76-mm guns and fortify the areas where they are located are told in the following article written by a Soviet artillery officer:

"Fortifying 45- and 76-mm gun positions is hard work, but it pays large dividends in combatting German tanks. Crews are taught not only to dig in and to camouflage quickly, but also to mine sectors in front of their batteries. When time permits, two or three alternate positions are dug for each gun and are used to confuse the enemy in spotting our gun positions. Artillery fire from these positions is also frequently imitated in order to draw enemy fire.

"Open positions are soon knocked out by enemy tanks or aircraft. Therefore, a platform with all-around traverse is built first. Beside it is dug a hole into which the gun may be lowered. Ditches, 1 1/2 yards deep, for personnel and ammunition, are dug on each side of the platform. The hole and the ditches are covered with logs, poles, and a 1/2-yard thickness of earth to guard against shell and bomb splinters. About 2 to 3 yards from the emplacement, another ditch is dug—this one for reserve ammunition. In battle, enemy tanks and planes make it very difficult to bring up additional ammunition from the rear. At some distance from the gun positions, dugouts 3 to 4 yards long and 2 yards wide, with inclined entrances, are dug for the horses. These dugouts are covered with poles, leaving a gap 1 to 1 1/2 feet wide to admit enough light to prevent restlessness.

"In the spring battles, the Red Army artillery was organized in depth. The 45-mm guns were emplaced on the front lines, and were protected by other antitank defenses. The crews were able to set up minefields in front of the gun positions, as well as obstacles, and also to lift the mines when necessary. In addition, each artillery battalion and, in some cases, each artillery battery, had a mobile reserve of 5 to 8 combat engineers equipped with 4 to 5 mines each. Their function was to mine unguarded tank approaches after the direction of the enemy attack had been definitely ascertained. These mines proved highly effective in stopping and even in destroying many enemy tanks."

c. Air Support

The Russians insist on thorough air reconnaissance to safeguard their forces—particularly infantry—from surprise tank attacks. If there is any possibility of a clash with enemy armor, mixed columns of infantry, artillery, and tanks are employed, closely supported by aircraft.

Russian close-support aircraft—including the highly respected Stormovik planes—often have achieved good results in attacking German tanks and other armored vehicles.

d. Use of Antitank Rifle

The following information about the use of the Russian antitank rifle was originally published in the Red Star, official Soviet Army publication:

"A Soviet artillery battery was on the march when the column was suddenly attacked by six enemy tanks. A Red Army private armed with an antitank rifle jumped off a caisson, took position behind a mound, and opened fire. He inflicted sufficient damage on the leading tank to cause the remainder of the enemy tanks to delay their attack for a few minutes. The battery was given a chance to deploy and open fire, and the surprise attack was beaten off. Four of the six German tanks were put out of action.

"In many similar instances antitank rifles have proved effective against enemy tanks. The light weight, portability, and rapid fire power of this weapon permit its crew to go into action in so short a time that it can cover units on the march, at rest, or in battle.

"...The greatest success has been attained by squads consisting of two or three antitank rifles placed 15 to 20 yards apart. Such units can bring effective fire to bear on a target, and have a greater chance of putting it out of commission than fire by a single rifle would have.

In selecting positions for antitank titles, detailed reconnaissance of the target area should be made, in addition to the usual local reconnaissance. Eliminating dead spots and protecting against the most likely routes of enemy tank approach are most important considerations. The positions should be echeloned so as to be mutually supporting with fire from the flanks. Antitank rifles in artillery batteries are generally grouped on the most exposed flank of the gun positions. In all cases, the squad leader should select his own position so as to have maximum observation and, at the same time, personally control the actions of the antitank rifles.

In fortifying these positions, it has proved impracticable to construct emplacements with roofs because of increased visibility to the enemy air force and lack of 360° traverse. The best types of emplacements are open and circular in shape, with a diameter large enough to permit free movement of the crew for all-around traverse and to protect the gun and crew from being crushed by enemy tanks. Narrow communication trenches connect the gun positions with each other as well as with the rear. Both emplacements and trenches are constructed without parapets; the extra dirt is utilized in building false installations to draw enemy fire. It is practically impossible for tanks to spot such fortifications, and the rifles are able to fire on them for the longest possible time.

Also, protection against aerial bombardment is increased.

"In the preparation of antitank fire, the rifleman should select five or six key reference points at different ranges, measure the distance to them, and study the intervening terrain. When actually firing, he should fire at stationary tanks whenever possible and not take leads at ranges over 400 yards. Aim should always be taken at the vulnerable parts, taking advantage of any hesitation or exposure of the sides of the enemy tanks.

"Antitank defense must be drawn up so as to protect the antitank rifle units fully, by means of all available obstacles, mines, and fire power."

e. Recent Trends

Recent trends in Russian antitank tactics are discussed in an article appearing in the "Red Star." An extract from this article follows:

Correctly disposed and camouflaged, antitank weapons can and do stop the German tanks. One case of a recent battle is recorded in which three antitank guns of the regimental artillery held off 56 German tanks in an all-day battle and destroyed 5. Another case records 35 to 40 German tanks attempting to cross a river, over a single bridge. One well-placed antitank gun destroyed 5 German tanks and forced the remainder to seek other means of crossing.

Communication with the chief of the artillery unit, with the infantry commander, and with adjacent units is usually by radio.

All artillery and antitank defenses are subordinated to the sector commander.

No set rule can be laid clown as to the density of antitank weapons on any sector. The system depends upon the terrain and the local situation. In general, there should be greater density toward the rear. An attack by a large number of tanks is met at the front lines by artillery and rifle fire. Then antitank rifles and destroyer tanks come into play. If the enemy tanks still break through, they run into tank obstacles defended by flanking and rear antitank fire. Soviet infantry at this point attempts to cut off the German infantry from its tank support. The enemy tanks then continue to run into tank destroyers and an increasing number of minefields.

Where Soviet tanks are used in the defense, they must not be pushed out front, but must be scattered to the rear and dug in to await a possible breakthrough, where they can do their best work.

More from the same series

Most books from the 'Eastern Front from Primary Sources' series are edited and endorsed by Emmy Award winning film maker and military historian Bob Carruthers, producer of Discovery Channel's Line of Fire and Weapons of War and BBC's Both Sides of the Line. Long experience and strong editorial control gives the military history enthusiast the ability to buy with confidence.

The series advisor is David McWhinnie, producer of the acclaimed Battlefield series for Discovery Channel. David and Bob have co-produced books and films with a wide variety of the UK's leading historians including Professor John Erickson and Dr David Chandler. Where possible the books draw on rare primary sources to give the military enthusiast new insights into a fascinating subject.

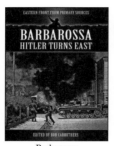

Barbarossa

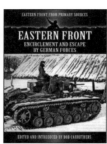

Eastern Front: Encirclement

Götterdämmerung

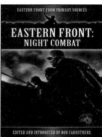

Eastern Front: Night Combat

The Waffen SS in the East 1941-1943

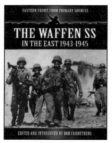

The Waffen SS in the East 1943-1945

The Wehrmacht Experience in Russia

Winter Warfare

The Red Army in Combat

Wehrmacht Combat Reports: The Russian Front

For more information visit www.pen-and-sword.co.uk